175
HIGH-IMPACT
COVER LETTERS

Richard H. Beatty

WILEY

John Wiley & Sons, Inc.

New York • Chichester • Brisbane • Toronto • Singapore

To the thousands of job applicants
who have sent me their cover letters over
the years, and whose letters have been used as the
basis for the sample letters contained in this book.
Thank you!

In recognition of the importance of preserving what has been written, it is a policy of John Wiley & Sons, Inc., to have books of enduring value published in the United States printed on acid-free paper, and we exert our best efforts to that end.

This publication is designed to provide accurate and authoritative information in regard to the subject matter covered. It is sold with the understanding that the publisher is not engaged in rendering legal, accounting, or other professional service. If legal advice or other expert assistance is required, the services of a competent professional person should be sought. *From a Declaration of Principles jointly adopted by a Committee of the American Bar Association and a Committee of Publishers.*

Library of Congress Cataloging-in-Publication Data

Beatty, Richard H., 1939–
    175 High-impact cover letters / by Richard H. Beatty.
      p.   cm.
    ISBN 0-471-55711-0 (alk. paper)
    IBSN 0-471-55712-9 (pbk.) (alk. paper)
    1. Cover letters. 2. Job hunting.   I. Title.
    HF5383.3323 1992
    650.14—dc20   91-36548

Printed in the United States of America

10 9 8 7 6

Contents

Preface

One of the most difficult chores of running a successful job-hunting campaign is writing effective cover letters. Unlike a resume, which the job seeker can spend hours perfecting, a cover letter must often be written "on the run" but still needs to be tailored to specific circumstances. For most people, this is not an easy task. And, unfortunately, in many cases a hurriedly prepared cover letter can lead to disastrous results!

The cover letter is far too important a document to be left to chance or to be written hurriedly at the last minute. Instead, the job seeker needs to be equipped ahead of time with an arsenal of highly effective, professional cover letter models that, with only minor modification, can be rapidly deployed as needed.

This book provides the job seeker with just such an arsenal! It contains 175 highly effective cover letter samples that, with slight modification, can be rapidly deployed by the job seeker throughout the job-hunting campaign. These letters have been designed to meet a wide range of circumstances that the job seeker will likely encounter and to equip him or her with the ability to quickly respond with a well-written, professional document that will create a favorable impression with employers and serve to enhance one's employment candidacy.

The reader is furnished with specific instructions and numerous model letters to assist in the preparation of five different types of cover letters: the employer broadcast letter, the search firm broadcast letter, the advertising response letter, the networking cover letter, and the increasingly popular resume letter. A full chapter, along with 30 or more model letters, has been dedicated to each of the five letter types.

The chapter on advertising response letters should prove particularly interesting and helpful. This chapter contains some thirty sample cover letters along with the sample advertisements that they were designed to answer. By comparing the sample cover letter to the corresponding advertisement, readers can quickly see how to construct an efficient and impactful letter that is highly tailored to the employer's specific requirements.

Also provided is a chapter on the popular resume letter, which is a cross between the cover letter and the resume. The resume letter is being used by the modern job seeker with increasing frequency as a replacement for the resume and is designed to be easy to read and to create interest in one's employment candidacy without forcing the employer to read the resume itself. If well designed, the resume letter can prove a highly effective job-search tool.

All in all, with the step-by-step instructions and 175 cover letter samples provided, this book should greatly simplify the chore of cover letter writing for most job seekers. It should provide readers with all of the ammunition necessary to write highly effective, professional cover letters that will substantially enhance the overall effectiveness of their job-hunting campaign.

Best wishes for a successful job search and a rewarding career.

RICHARD H. BEATTY

West Chester, Pennsylvania
March 1992

1

Importance of Cover Letters

The cover letter, which accompanies your employment resume, can clearly be a most critical tool to the overall effectiveness of your job search. If carefully thought out and well-designed, it can be analogous to the well-designed cover of a good book—attracting attention, raising curiosity, compelling interest, and begging the reader to read on.

If well-designed, well-written, and informative, the cover letter can do much to grab the reader's attention, raise his curiosity, and greatly stimulate interest in your employment candidacy. In fact, if exceptionally well written, the cover letter can sometimes even stimulate sufficient interest in your credentials to convince the recipient that you are a highly desirable candidate worthy of an employment interview—without his even bothering to read the resume that accompanies it.

By contrast, the poorly written cover letter can be absolutely disastrous to an otherwise successful job-hunting campaign. The way this letter is organized, "what" it says, "how" it is stated, what is included/excluded, what is highlighted/emphasized—all are critical factors to the effectiveness of the cover letter. Those that are poorly conceived and fail to give due consideration to these important factors can (and will) be fatal to your employment candidacy—causing the reader to discard your resume with no further thought given to your candidacy whatsoever.

As an employment professional with a number of years of experience, I have never ceased to be amazed at the fact that some people will put hours (or even days) into the preparation and design of the "perfect" resume—one that impressively highlights their qualifications and skillfully markets their credentials—then put only five minutes preparation time into a cover letter that causes them to "fall flat on their face." Such behavior simply defies all logic and rules of basic common sense.

Let's face it; the cover letter is the first thing that meets the reader's eye. And we have all heard and read a great deal about the importance of "first impressions" in the employment and interview process. Well, the cover letter is no exception! It is the document that creates that all-important "first impression," and it will have a great deal of impact on how the reader "perceives" you right from the start.

If the cover letter is neat and well written, it will clearly create a positive impression and suggest that you are someone who is neat and careful about your work. By contrast, a sloppy or poorly written cover letter will suggest that you are someone who has little regard for the quality of your work.

Besides cover letter appearance, "what" you say in the cover letter (and "how" you say it) can have considerable impact on the reader. These factors immediately tell the reader something about your general communication skills. For example, they can telegraph to the reader whether you are expressive, concise, articulate—or whether you are inexpressive, overly detailed, inarticulate, or worse. These factors (that is, "what" you say and "how" you say it) can also telegraph to the reader something about your intellectual capacity and how you think. For example, these factors can suggest to the reader that you are someone who is conceptual, strategic, analytical, logical, and the like or (if the letter is not carefully choreographed) that you are someone whose thinking is muddled, overly simplistic, illogical, disorganized, or even worse.

Finally, if well designed, the cover letter can do a lot to "premarket" your candidacy. If, as a result of reading your cover letter, for example, the reader is feeling positive and impressed with what you have to say, these feelings will likely spill over into the resume, which will then be read with a far less critical eye. Conversely, if the cover letter is poorly designed, your resume may not get read at all.

Although it is difficult for me to believe as an employment professional, I have had prominent people tell me that they place more stock in the cover letter than they do in the resume. Some have, in fact, told me that they have invited certain candidates in for employment interviews based solely on the strength of their cover letters, without regard to the resumes. Amazingly, some of these same individuals have even volunteered that they seldom bother to read the resume if the cover letter is impressive.

So, considering the overwhelming evidence, one doesn't have to be a rocket scientist to come to the conclusion that the cover letter is a very important document indeed. How it is designed and written can clearly make a significant difference in the success of one's job-hunting campaign. Your cover letters clearly deserve your deliberate and careful attention if you are serious about maximizing your opportunities in the marketplace. This book, if carefully followed, should therefore provide you with a distinct competitive advantage.

TYPES OF COVER LETTERS

When most people think about cover letters, they have in mind the letter that is used to transmit their resume to a prospective employer. Actually, there are five types of cover letters, each designed a little differently and each having a slightly different purpose:

1. Letters to Employers
2. Letters to Search Firms
3. Advertising Response Letters
4. Networking Cover Letters
5. Resume Letters

The ensuing chapters of this book are designed to thoroughly familiarize you with each of these letter types and to provide you with numerous examples as the basis for modeling and writing your own effective cover letters. By carefully studying these sample letters, along with the instructions provided at the beginning of each chapter, you should have all you need to write a highly effective cover letter and add a good deal of zest and positive impact to your job-hunting campaign.

2

Letters to Employers

If you are contemplating use of a mass mailing program to send your resume to employers, you need to know that you are playing a "numbers game." Although a standard element of most well-planned job-hunting campaigns, such mass mailings have not been known for producing significant results when compared to the use of more productive job-hunting sources, such as networking, recruitment advertising, and employment agencies. Nonetheless, should you elect to use the direct-mail approach, you will need an effective cover letter if you wish to realize a reasonable return on the time you invest in this process.

Professionals who specialize in the direct-mail business have long known that, if well prepared, a direct-mail campaign will generally generate a return in the 3 to 5 percent range. Thus, a targeted mailing of 300 letters should be expected to generate only 9 to 15 responses. So, if you are planning to utilize this approach as part of your job search program, you will want to be thinking of making a sizable mailing that will target several hundred firms.

In a tight labor market, characterized by high unemployment and a glut of candidates available on the market, the direct-mail approach can be even less effective. Recent research conducted during such a market, for example, has shown a positive response rate of only 3 percent. Further, some knowledgeable employment experts feel that the rate of return is likely even lower than this, depending upon the severity of employment market conditions.

When you consider whether or not to utilize direct mail as part of your job-hunting program, the important thing to remember, however, is that it takes only a *single* favorable response to generate a job interview. If it's the right job, this approach can pay off rather handsomely, providing you with the chance to move forward with an exciting and rewarding career opportunity.

So don't be overly discouraged by the somewhat meager statistical results cited here. Instead, be sure to make the direct-mail campaign to employers one of the components of your job search plan. Just don't be overly optimistic about the volume of expected result.

THE BROADCAST LETTER

In the parlance of employment professionals, the cover letter used by job seekers to transmit their resumes to prospective employers is commonly known as a *broadcast* letter. This name comes from the idea that the letter is used to broadcast the candidate's employment availability to a large audience.

Clearly the composition of the broadcast letter will be extremely important to the outcome of your direct-mail campaign. If well designed and well written, it will improve your response rate and substantially increase the number of interview opportunities presented to you. Conversely, if poorly designed or poorly written, it will detract from your mailing results and reduce (or even eliminate) your opportunities for employment interviews.

So, if you are going to assure yourself of an effective direct-mail campaign, you will want to spend some quality time in designing a well-written cover letter that will successfully market your skills and capabilities to prospective employers.

LIST OF TARGET COMPANIES

Wherever possible, your broadcast cover letter should be directed to a specific individual at each of the target firms that you have selected. Research has demonstrated that such "personally targeted" mailings are looked upon more favorably by recipients, and that this practice will measurably increase the probability of a favorable response. Quite frankly, a letter simply addressed to the "Manager of Manufacturing," without use of that individual's name, does not engender warm feelings on the part of the recipient and "just doesn't cut it" if you expect to maximize the results of your mailing campaign!

When you research your list of target companies, therefore, it is imperative that you take the time to find the name and exact title of the individual whom you wish to target. The rule of thumb for deciding who that person should be is to select the individual who is managerially one step above the person for whom you would likely work in that particular firm. When it is not possible for you to identify that person, then choose the top executive listed for the functional area you have chosen as your target.

Printed sources that list this kind of personnel information are not always easily identified. If you are in a quandary about where to go to identify directories that provide the names and titles of the key personnel whom you wish to target, the national offices of industry or professional associations have frequently proven to be helpful. By calling the association's president, you can frequently identify publications (which are either industry- or profession-specific) that provide the kind of in-depth personnel information you will need to prepare an effective mailing list.

THE CARDINAL RULE

When you are preparing your direct-mail program, one cardinal rule to follow is "Never mail your cover letter and resume to the personnel (or employment) department!" These departments are normally inundated with unsolicited resumes and are many times simply not staffed or equipped to efficiently handle the volume of employment mail received. This is especially true during recent years when, due to corporate downsizing, staff functions such as personnel have had their resources cut drastically.

Additionally, it is important to realize that the personnel (or employment) function is frequently only aware of the organization's "formal" openings. That is, they are aware only of those employment openings that have been formally approved by management for hiring purposes. By contrast, they may be totally unaware of "informal" or "hidden" employment openings—those that are in the minds of their client managers and have not yet been formally communicated.

This phenomenon of "informal" employment openings has been dubbed the "hidden job market" by the professional employment community. Estimates by knowledgeable employment professionals suggest that the size of this hidden job market is such that it comprises some 70 to 80 percent of the entire job market. It is also said that these "hidden" jobs are most often filled long before they have a chance to become known to the general public through recruitment advertising, employment agencies, search firms, and the like.

Targeting your mailing directly to functional managers, rather than the personnel (or employment) department, thus gives you the opportunity to access this hidden job market. Receipt of your broadcast cover letter, along with accompanying resume, could be just the trigger mechanism to generate an interview rather than a standard "no interest" form letter from the firm's personnel department.

You can now see why it is so important to target your letters to specific line managers if you wish to maximize the results of your direct mail program.

THE VALUE-ADDED CONCEPT

When you are designing your general broadcast cover letter, it is imperative to bear in mind that employers don't fill positions just for the sake of filling them. Obviously, they are looking for candidates who are capable of accomplishing specific results—persons who can "add value" to their organizations.

Some careful analysis of the job content of your targeted position (job search objective) should yield some awfully good clues of the type of results (and value) employers expect of a successful candidate. Good cover letter design will serve to highlight your ability to contribute specific results and add value in these important areas. The following exercise should help you to define these areas:

1. What are the key, ongoing functional accountabilities of the position for which you are applying?
2. In each of these key functional areas, what are the end results that are likely to be desired by the employer?
3. What important results have you achieved in each of these key areas that would be of interest to the employer and could serve to communicate your "value" to the employer?

In those cases in which you are just entering the job market for the first time, you will need a slightly different approach. In this event, you will want to focus on specific skills and attributes you possess that should enable you to perform the job particularly well. Perhaps the following questions may help you to organize your thoughts on this matter.

1. What are the key problems you will need to solve if you are to be successful in performing your targeted job?
2. What key knowledge and/or skills will be required in order for you to solve these problems and achieve successful job performance?
3. Which of these qualifications (knowledge/skills) do you possess?
4. What evidence can you cite of your ability to apply these key factors?
5. What personal attributes are thought to be important to successful performance of your targeted job?
6. Which of these do you possess?
7. What evidence can you cite of this?

The sample cover letters contained in this chapter will effectively illustrate how these key accomplishments or important personal traits can be highlighted to your best advantage.

KEY ELEMENTS OF BROADCAST LETTER

Review of the sample cover letters provided in this chapter will also reveal that there are five key elements to effective broadcast cover letter composition:

1. An introductory paragraph, which includes a statement of your job search objective
2. A brief summary paragraph, which summarizes your overall background and experience
3. A "selling" (value-adding) paragraph, which highlights specific results achieved by you in those areas known to be important to successful job performance
4. A request for action on your candidacy
5. A statement of appreciation for the employer's consideration of your employment candidacy

You will note these key elements in the following cover letter samples, which have been provided as the basis for modeling your own effective direct-mail cover letters.

HAROLD D. FOX

8000 Burlingame Avenue
Atlanta, GA 53825

Office: (214) 837-5070
Home: (214) 977-5642

April 21, 1994

Ms. Sarah R. Dixon
Engineering Manager
Lexitron, Inc.
123 Seabright Road
Provident, RI 73692

Dear Ms. Dixon:

I am interested in a position as a Project Engineer with Lexitron, Inc. Review of my resume will reveal that I have strong project experience with Johnnan Corporation, one of your key competitors.

I graduated with a B.S. degree in Mechanical Engineering from Princeton University, and have 6 years of paper machine project experience. I enjoy an excellent reputation for bringing projects in on time and at or below budget. Some key project experience includes:

- Completion of a $54 million twin wire, forming section rebuild project on time and under budget ($1.2 million savings)

- Lead wet end Project Engineer for purchase, design and installation of a new $150 million Beloit paper machine ($120K savings)

- Engineered, installed, and started-up $45 million rebuild of after dryer section of twin wire tissue machine (project completed 2 months ahead of schedule with savings of $1/2 million)

Although well-versed in most machine configurations, I am especially knowledgeable of twin wire formers and some of the newer, state-of-the-art sheet forming technology. These qualifications could prove very additive to those companies interested in upgrading their overall papermaking technology.

If you are currently seeking a strong paper machine project engineer, I would appreciate the opportunity to further discuss my qualifications with you. Thank you for your consideration.

Sincerely yours,

Harold D. Fox

Harold D. Fox

HDF/dar
Enclosure

127 South Bend Road
Cleveland, Ohio 47397
January 29, 1996

Mr. Donald R. Smith
Director of Marketing
Delro Foods Company
100 East River Road
Portland, Oregon 26718

Dear Mr. Smith:

I am writing to present my credentials for the position of Brand Manager, a position for which I am exceptionally well-qualified. I am confident that you will quickly realize my ability to make major contributions to Delro Foods' marketing efforts upon reviewing the enclosed resume.

As my resume will attest, I have established an excellent reputation for pumping new life into old brands and making them perform. Examples of my accomplishments in this area are:

- Doubled Pikkels market share in only 9 months

- Increased Yums market share by 99% in two years

- Improved direct mail orders of Beard's Sunframes by 38% in 18 months through use of creative coupons

My contributions to new brands have been equally noteworthy. For example:

- Achieved 29% market share penetration for Leggins within one year of market introduction.

- Completed national roll-out of Jelli-Roll in 6 months, reaching 18% market penetration

Perhaps I can make similar contributions to Delro Foods in the marketing of either new or existing brands.

Should you have room in your organization for a top-notch marketing professional who is capable of making immediate contributions to your marketing efforts and adding some real profit to your bottom line, please give me a call. I look forward to hearing from you.

Thank you for your consideration.

Sincerely,

Weldon R. Bass

Weldon R. Bass

WRB/crs

Enclosure

122 Wheaton Hall
Syracuse University
Syracuse, NY 29483
February 10, 1994

Ms. Beverly M. Radon
Director of Marketing and Sales
Bardon Corporation
Suite 330, Winton Towers
133 East 22nd Street
Chicago, IL 19835

Dear Ms. Radon:

I am very interested in talking with you about employment as a Sales Representative Trainee with Bardon Corporation, and hope you will give my candidacy strong consideration. I feel I have the necessary skills and interest to be an excellent contributor to your organization, and would like the opportunity to demonstrate this through a personal interview with your recruiter during Bardon Corporation's forthcoming recruiting schedule at Syracuse. My resume is enclosed for your reference.

Although short on experience, Ms. Radon, I am long on effort and enthusiasm. I am an outgoing, friendly individual who would enjoy building strong interpersonal relationships with valued customers. My strong service orientation and bias for action would serve your company well in responding to the needs and concerns of your clients. My drive, determination and leadership abilities are well-evidenced by the following accomplishments:

- Grade Point Average of 3.7/4.0

- Fraternity President, Senior Year
  Fraternity Vice President, Junior Year
  Pledge Chairman, Sophomore Year

- Captain, Varsity Crew Team, Senior Year
  Member, Varsity Crew Team, 3 Years
  Co-Captain, Varsity Swim Team, Junior Year
  Member, Varsity Swim Team, 4 Years

I would like the chance to put my energy, drive and enthusiasm to work for a company such as yours. May I have the opportunity to further discuss your requirements during a personal meeting with your representative on February 22nd?

Sincerely,

Nicholas C. Burkholder

NCB/rab

Enclosure

SANDRA A. SYMINGTON
400 East Butternut Lane
Lansdale, Pennsylvania 19385

May 18, 1995

Mr. John C. Lupton
President and CEO
Farber Industries, Inc.
100 North Hill Road
Denver, CO 19774

Dear Mr. Lupton:

As the executive officer of a leading company in the copper industry, I am sure that you are well aware of the value of a top-notch manufacturing executive to a profit-oriented company. If you are currently seeking a proven contributor to lead your manufacturing operations, I encourage you to give serious consideration to my credentials.

As a manufacturing executive with an M.S. degree in Engineering and over 15 years of solid achievement and career progression, I have established a distinguished reputation as a strong profit contributor. Among some of my more notable accomplishments are:

- a 36% reduction in manufacturing costs in a major furnace operation (annual savings of $13 million)

- on time and below cost start-up of a $435 million tube manufacturing plant (project savings of $7 million)

- a 28% reduction in labor costs over a three-plant operation through extensive work redesign project (annual savings of $5.9 million)

- a 68% reduction in scrap and 86% reduction in customer complaints through implementation of a SPC-based total quality effort (Annual savings of $4.8 million)

Perhaps we should meet to discuss the contributions that I could make to your firm if employed as a senior member of your manufacturing team. Should you agree, I can be reached during office hours at (215) 887-2391 or at (215) 334-7851 in the evening.

Sincerely,

Sandra A. Symington

Sandra A. Symington

SAS/drm

Enclosure

526 Ogdon Road
Springfield, MA 28472
October 26, 1996

Dr. Sheldon P. Worthington
Vice President of Research
Farley Chemical Company
825 Skinner Blvd.
Houston, TX 28736

Dear Dr. Worthington:

Farley Chemical Company, as one of the leaders in the field of polymer chemistry, might be interested in a seasoned Product Development Chemist with a demonstrated record of achievement as a new product innovator. My credentials include an M.S. in Polymer Chemistry with over 15 years research experience in the polymer industry.

As you can see from the enclosed resume, my reputation as a creative, innovative contributor is well supported by some 22 registered patents and an additional 18 patent disclosures. My work has led to the successful introduction of 12 new products which now account for over $250 million in annual sales revenues.

I have extensive experience in the following specialty areas:

Organic & Polymer Specialty Chemicals:
- Water Treatment Chemicals
- Oil Field & Mining Chemicals
- Consumer Products Based on Water Soluble Polymers

Polymers, Rubbers and Plastics:
- New Polymers and Plastics - Synthetic Approach
- New Polymers and Plastics - Physio-Chemical Approach

My current salary is $82,000, and I have no geographical restrictions.

Should you have an appropriate opportunity available as a member of your research staff, Dr.Worthington, I would welcome the opportunity to meet with you to discuss the contributions that I might make to your new product development efforts. I can be reached during evening hours at (313) 528-9375.

Thank you for your consideration, and I look forward to hearing from you.

Sincerely yours,

Walter D. Paxton

WDP/ssr

Enclosure

BARBARA A. ANDERSON
1220 Briar Patch Path
Carlton Woods, WA 18882
(218) 377-0895

March 15, 1993

Mr. Keith B. Cunningham
Vice President of Human Resources
Earth Sciences Corporation
1000 Kentucky Ridge Parkway
Williamstown, KY 34729

Dear Mr. Cunningham:

Enclosed please find my resume for the position of Director of Employment. Should you have an opening at this level, I am confident that you will find my qualifications intriguing.

My credentials include an M.S. in Industrial Relations from Michigan State University with 14 years of solid human resources experience. This includes nearly 9 years in the employment function - 6 as Manager of Administrative Employment with Drexel Electronics, Inc. and nearly 3 years as a National Practice Director for Russell J. Reynolds, a premiere international executive search consulting firm.

I have also managed a Fortune 200 employment function with responsibility for recruitment of executive, managerial and professional employees for a wide range of functional areas. I enjoy a strong reputation for cost-effective, timely and quality recruitment, and am thoroughly versed in state-of-the-art behavioral-based interviewing and assessment methodology.

If you seek a knowledgeable professional to manage your corporate employment function, I hope that you will give me a call so that we may discuss your requirements and the contributions that I can make to your company.

Sincerely

Barbara A. Anderson

Barbara A. Anderson

BAA/rem

Enclosure

WALTER C. WASHINGTON

300 PORTER WAY
CLEARVIEW, OR 13728

HOME: (313) 577-5512
OFFICE: (313) 988-4432

August 19, 1997

Mr. Cleon C. Carter
Manager of Corporate Accounting
General Electronics Company
800 Cleveland Way
Greenville, NC 18472

Dear Mr. Carter:

I am writing to apply for the position of Cost Accountant in your Corporate Accounting Department. I feel that I have excellent qualifications for this position, and would appreciate your careful consideration of the enclosed resume.

A 1990 graduate of Villanova University with a B.S. in Accounting, I have over 7 years of employment in the Accounting profession. This includes some 4 years as an Auditor with Price Waterhouse and another 3 years as a Cost Accountant with the Burlington Corporation. I have received excellent professional training and, throughout my career, as copies of past performance evaluations will attest, I have consistently attained the highest ratings possible.

Current annual compensation is $65,000, and I would expect a competitive increase in keeping with my qualifications and experience level.

Although open to relocation, my preference is for the Southeast. Other locations may be of interest dependent upon the specifics of the opportunity.

If you feel that your Corporate Accounting Department could benefit from the contributions of a seasoned, knowledgeable Cost Accountant, I would appreciate hearing from you. I can be reached during normal business hours at (418) 335-7335.

Thank you for your consideration, and I look forward to hearing from you.

Sincerely yours,

Walter C. Washington

Walter C. Washington

Enclosure

PATRICIA M. WAVERLY
135 East Wilson Drive
Flint, Michigan 25371
(313) 966-1757

May 24, 1997

Mr. David P. Ducket
Chief Financial Officer
Rathyeon Company
600 Industry Blvd.
Hillsboro, MA 98271

Dear Mr. Ducket:

If you are currently in the market for an accomplished Senior Financial Analyst who has established an excellent reputation for successful acquisition analysis, the enclosed resume should prove interesting to you.

My credentials include an M.B.A. in Finance from the University of Chicago and over 6 years acquisition analysis with the Business Development Department of a Fortune 100 food company. During this period I completed analysis of 28 acquisition candidates, which resulted in the acquisition of 6 highly profitable companies. These included:

- a $40 million acquisition of a baking company that has achieved
  an average ROI of 18% for the first 3 years of ownership

- a $28 million acquisition of a foods distribution company
  showing a 22% ROI in the 3rd year of operation

- a $62 million purchase of a food wrap company that yielded
  a 12% return during first year following acquisition

Importantly, all acquisitions have proven highly profitable, with the poorest performer achieving an ROI of 8.2%. Additionally, all acquisitions were completed at a very attractive price-to-net-profit ratio.

Mr. Ducket, I would welcome the opportunity to meet with you personally to discuss the kinds of contributions I might make to Raytheon Company as a member of its Business Development staff.

If you see this as a worthwhile investment, I can be reached on a confidential basis at (313) 877-9075 during the day, or at my home phone during the evening.

Very truly yours,

Patricia A. Waverly

Patricia A. Waverly

Enclosure

DAVID C. JORDAN

816 Pintail Cliffs
Woodlawn, CO 18263

Home: (216) 886-5147
Office:(216) 872-9731

October 16, 1995

Ms. Katherine P. Walters
Senior Vice President - Administration
Cord & Decker, Inc.
18 Summerdale Court
Wolfgang Industrial Center
Ridgewood, NJ 16225

Dear Ms. Walters:

As the senior administrative executive for Cord & Decker, Inc., perhaps you are in need of a talented Purchasing Manager who can almost certainly make immediate contributions to the bottom line of your company.

A Senior Purchasing Agent for a Fortune 200, $2.8 billion consumer products company, I have enjoyed a reputation as a "tough but fair negotiator", who has made significant cost savings contributions to my employer. These have included:

- consolidated corporate-wide packaging supplies purchases with resultant annual savings of $35 million

- contributed $12 million annual savings through conversion from oil to biomass fuels with long-term purchase contract

- saved $8 million annually in inventory costs through installation of computerized raw materials tracking and forecasting system

- successfully negotiated five-year knock-down carton contract with major supplier worth $5.5 million savings annually

Educational credentials include a B.S. in Packaging from Michigan State University and an M.B.A. in Finance from Penn State University. I have more than 15 years purchasing experience with a major international corporation, and have been professionally active in my field.

Compensation requirements are in the low $80K range, and I am open to relocation anywhere in the United States.

Should you feel my background qualifies me for a current corporate management assignment at Cord & Decker, Inc., I would welcome the opportunity to meet with you. Please contact me at my home in the evening.

I appreciate your consideration.

Sincerely,

David C. Jordan

144 Baston Lane
Homeward, IL 27186
August 29, 1994

Mr. Frederick R. Wickard
Director of MIS
Whitingford, Inc.
100 Shining Way
Rosewood Corporate Center
Tampa, FL 27369

Dear Mr. Wickard:

As today's economy and competitive pressures place tighter constraints on business, IT professionals with a diverse background can provide greater value when budgets are tight.

As a versatile MIS professional, I have experience in project management for a wide variety of business applications in systems and database design, quality assurance, troubleshooting and programming. My B.B.A. in Accounting has given me an exceptional understanding of financial applications.

While at Johnson Corporation, my hands-on management style and strong technical skills have enabled me to meet deadlines in high pressured environments.

I am seeking a position in applications management developing business systems, or a liaison position between IT and the user community.

My current compensation is $65,000. Should you have an appropriate opening which parallels my background, I would appreciate a personal interview. I look forward to hearing from you.

Thank you for considering my credentials.

Very truly yours,

Sandra B. Timpkins

SBT/ram

Enclosure

CAROLYN A. BEATTY

400 East 7th Street
Lansdale, PA 19407

Home: (215) 557-0973
Office: (215) 883-2929

April 18, 1997

Ms. Janet N. Morse
Vice President of Human Resources
The Utica Corporation
100 Woodlawn Avenue
Utica, NY 27716

Dear Ms. Morse:

I am currently seeking a position as Training and Development Manager for a medium-sized manufacturing company. I am a hands-on, results-oriented leader with a comprehensive background in training design, development and delivery. The enclosed resume details the specifics of my experience and accomplishments.

My background spans over ten years of diverse training and development experience, providing support to a variety of functional clients. In all cases I have been successful in getting strong client support and ownership of the programs delivered. The following highlights some of my key accomplishments:

- Directed training of 200 person field sales organization for a major electronics distribution company

- Used assessment methodology as the basis for constructing "high performance models" for certain key management jobs. Assessed key managers against these models as the basis for defining key management development needs/priorities.

- Designed and delivered company's first highly successful introductory course to total quality management -- over 500 managers trained across 3 divisions.

- Developed methodology for linking training needs with business strategy, and put in place a reliable method for providing quantitative measurement of the effectiveness of management training and development programs.

Based upon my job experience and educational qualifications, I am confident that I can bring effective leadership to your training function and improve the overall human resource effectiveness and productivity of your company. I would appreciate the opportunity to further discuss my credentials with you during a face-to-face interview.

I hope to hear from you shortly.

Yours very truly,

Carolyn A. Beatty

Carolyn A Beatty

CAB/rhb

Enclosure

WENDEL B. THOMAS
145 Donovan Court
Ridge Pike Apartments
Mobile, AL 18337

November 12, 1997

Mr. Walter Chamberlaine
Vice President
Environmental Affairs Department
International Chemical Company
500 Park Avenue
New York, NY 17229

Dear Mr. Chamberlaine:

I am seeking a position where I can apply my experience as an environmental specialist. As an Environmental Project Manager in the Environmental Affairs Department of the Dow Chemical Company, I have gained experience in many areas of the environmental industry, especially hazardous substance and waste management as well as environmental legislation and compliance requirements.

Specific areas of accomplishment include:

- Company compliance with applicable local, state, and federal environmental regulations nationwide

- Design and implementation of training programs to limit company risk and liability in the hazardous substance management field

- Research and evaluation of cost-effective methods for hazardous substance reduction, recycling and conservation.

I am interested in an industry position in environmental compliance, hazardous substance management, and/or industrial environmental training and education. I am interested in a company that has a strong interest in developing pro-active programs to limit liability and risk in environmental affairs.

My resume is enclosed. Thank you for reviewing my credentials, and I look forward to hearing from you.

Sincerely,

Wendel B. Thomas

WBT/rer

Enclosure

RANDOLPH B. MANNINGTON

300 East Chaddsford Lane
Briarwood, NY 18337

Home: (315) 888-7755
Office: (212) 622-0471

January 20, 1995

Mr. Richard C. Courtsworth
Chairman of the Board
Bainsroth Chemical, Inc.
300 Industrial Parkway, South
Atlanta, GA 28395

Dear Mr. Courtsworth:

I am seeking a CEO position in the chemical industry. My professional career exhibits a record of strong achievement and significant contributions. I am a top performing chemical industry executive with an extensive sales, manufacturing, research and operations background.

Throughout my career, I recruited, selected and developed very talented managers. I utilized persistence, technical expertise and interpersonal skills to establish and build long-term relationships with diverse customers. I analyzed, evaluated and led entry into new market niches enabling the company to generate significant profits, and am recognized as a creative manager with strong strategic planning, communications, listening, and operational skills. The following highlight some of my key accomplishments:

- Analyzed markets, determined special market niches, shifted product line and aggressively led entry into new markets resulting in sales growth of 300% and a sizeable profit improvement ($5 million to $13.5 million).

- Exercised operational P&L responsibility for a $30 million corporation manufacturing industrial specialty O.E.M. paints and coatings.

- Landed major industrial accounts (Budd/Jeep Wrangler, Clarke Equipment, Caterpillar Trailer, Strick, and Fruehauf) by building solid relationships through persistent and creative presentations, development of superior products, and quality service.

If my qualifications are of interest, Mr. Courtsworth, I would be delighted to meet with you to further explore opportunities with your fine company. I hope that we will have the opportunity to meet shortly, and I look forward to hearing from you.

Sincerely,

Randolph B. Mannington

RBM/ctr

Enclosure

WILMA A. DAVIDSON
102 Senneca Drive
Fairlawn, NJ 18227

March 15, 1994

Mr. Stephen R. Troutsman
Vice President MIS
Tri Star Manufacturing, Inc.
600 Commerce Street
Newark, NJ 18223

Dear Mr. Troutsman:

Enclosed is my resume outlining more than 15 years extensive experience in corporate telecommunications. In summary, my credentials include:

- broad experience in international computer networking

- design and implementation of voice, data and LAN systems

- in-depth experience with telecommunications and information processing technologies

- interpersonal skills for interfacing well with all levels of management

I would like to put this expertise to work in a senior telecommunications management and/or internal consulting position.

Although I am concentrating my search in the greater New York City area, I would consider other locations for the right opportunity.

If you are currently searching for someone with my credentials, I would be pleased to meet with you to discuss I how might help you to solve some of your more difficult telecommunications problems. Thank you for your consideration.

Sincerely,

Wilma A. Davidson

Enclosure

WADE B. STANFORD

300 Breakers Lane
Ocean Reefs, CA 16772

Home: (309) 557-8925
Office: (309) 874-2111

May 20, 1996

Ms. Denise K. MacQueen
Director of Sales
DMR Corporation
300 Computer Court
Kingston Corporate Center
Daleville, TX 17337

Dear Ms. MacQueen:

Are you looking for a salesperson for the information processing industry? Maybe I can help you.

I am the corporate representative for twenty major customers at IBM Corporation. Based on this experience I can:

- Meet large global customers' total information systems requirements

- Negotiate worldwide volume purchase agreements

- Sell in international markets

- Respond to the concerns of senior management

- Leverage all corporate resources to achieve customer satisfaction

Although other factors such as career growth are of primary importance to me, you should know that my total compensation is $75,000.

I appreciate your consideration.

Very truly yours,

Wade B. Stanford

WBS/fah

Enclosure

133 Lakeview Drive
Detroit, MI 16226
June 22, 1997

Ms. Barbara T. Swainsforth
Director Research & Development
Roofing Division
Kelco Corporation
222 Railroad Avenue
Grand Rapids, MI 17266

Dear Ms. Swainsforth:

I am a registered engineer in the state of Michigan, and I am presently seeking a position in the roofing industry. A copy of my resume is enclosed, and I would like to talk with you should you have an appropriate opportunity for me at Kelco Corporation.

My most recent assignment was to manage projects at Forte Products Company to develop products for the commercial roofing industry. Part of my responsibility was to provide technical support to sales people, when they had questions of a technical nature from their engineering or architectural customers.

I have experience in quality assurance and the application of control charting to a large insulation line at Forte Products. This resulted in a 23% reduction in scrap and a 76% reduction in customer complaints.

I am seeking a position as a team leader or manager in product or process development, or in quality assurance. My compensation requirements are in the $65,000 to $70,000 range, and I am open to relocation.

I would welcome the opportunity to talk with you and discuss the technical contributions I could make to the Kelco Corporation, especially in the development of exciting new roofing products.

Thank you for reviewing my credentials, and I look forward to hearing from you shortly.

Sincerely,

James C. Willison

Enclosure

WANDA R. RICHARDSON
325 West Rosedale Avenue
Denver, CO 17344

April 16, 1994

Mr. Reed W. Carter
Director of Quality
General Electric Company
200 Electric Drive
Troy, NY 17729

Dear Mr. Carter:

I am seeking a position as a Facilitator for Total Quality Management in a firm already using TQM, or one just beginning TQM implementation.

Beginning with BS and MS degrees in engineering and following with 15 years experience with Westinghouse, I have built a solid career foundation in shop operations, manufacturing engineering and plant management.

Three years ago I became convinced of the potential of Total Quality Management and began some TQM initiatives with the Electric Motors Division. This proved highly successful but, due to recent budget cutbacks, many of the resources targeted for further implementation of these programs have been temporarily frozen.

I am now seeking an opportunity to continue my efforts with a company that has a firm commitment to Total Quality implementation. I have much to contribute, and would welcome the change.

Should you have an appropriate opening on your quality management staff, I would appreciate the opportunity to explore employment possibilities with you. Thank you for your consideration.

Sincerely,

Wanda R. Richardson

Wanda R. Richardson

WRR/smt

Enclosure

WALLACE T. BARRINGTON

600 Buckingham Lane   Home: (908) 775-0902
Princeton, NJ 19847   Office: (908) 775-8725

April 10, 1994

Mr. Donald D. Travis
President
Weldon Energy Corporation
1110 West Industry Blvd.
Cleveland, Ohio 17328

Dear Mr. Travis:

Please take 60 seconds to consider a senior executive who has:

- Directed operations of eight international manufacturing
  companies with a combined sales volume of $120 million.

- Increased profits by 40%, reduced late deliveries by 76%
  and increased market share by 15%..

- As a CFO, arranged debt and equity financings, implemented
  new manufacturing and accounting systems for a firm that
  grew from $18 million to $160 million in 20 months.

- As a consultant, created corporate strategy for a $6
  billion company.

- MBA from Harvard and BS Engineering from Princeton

- High energy, excellent interpersonal skills and experience
  to meet challenging opportunities such as rapid growth,
  business decline and turnaround situations.

Should you have room on your senior management staff and can use my qualifications, please
contact me so that we can meet personally. Thank you.

Sincerely,

Wallace T. Barrington

WTB/dap

Enclosure

KAREN J. ROBINSON
155 North Bank Road
Lakeview, WA 17385
(216) 775-0245

June 26, 1998

Mr. Harold D. Klein
Vice President Operations
Redding Beverage Company
345 West Front Street
Allentown, PA 19472

Dear Mr. Klein:

I am seeking an Operations Management position at the plant, division or corporate level with a major player in the food and beverage industry. Please consider my credentials.

As my resume will show, I have had excellent progression in the field of Operations Management with one of the top U.S. consumer products companies. Pepsi-Cola, as you may know, has been ranked by <u>Fortune</u> magazine among the top 6 best run companies in America.

In my current position as Group Plant Manager (3 plants) for Pepsi West, I have been credited with annual cost savings exceeding $2 million as the result of several innovative cost reduction programs recently implemented. I have just been awarded Pesi's coveted "High Performer Award" for my contributions.

Prior assignments have been equally productive, and I have consistently demonstrated the ability to achieve superior results. I pride myself on staying current in all major new developments in the field of Operations and push hard for the implementation of those that will readily increase ease of operations and reduce operating costs.

Should you be in the market for a proven contributor as a member of your Operations Team, Mr. Klein, your time would be well spent in meeting with me. Much of what I have already done at Pepsi might well be transferable to Redding Beverage, and could result in substantial savings to your company.

Should you wish to contact me, I can be reached during the day at (216) 377-0925, or at the above number during evening hours.

Thank you for your consideration.

Sincerely,

Karen J. Robinson

Karen J. Robinson

KJR/tag

Enclosure

P.O. Box 525
Wayland, TX 17263
March 12, 1995

Darrel H. Johnston
Senior Vice President
Technology Division
Texas Telecom, Inc.
300 Arlington Drive
Dallas, TX 28495

Dear Mr. Johnston:

Attached is my resume. I am currently seeking a Director level position in the Technical Services area. My background is predominantly Telecommunications with areas of expertise in Training, Publications, and Field Service.

If you feel that my resume warrants consideration for opportunities at Texas Telecom, please contact me at (214) 816-9402 or (903) 635-9576.

Thank you for your time and consideration.

Sincerely,

Kevin T. Langsford

KTL/rbs

Enclosure

TYLER W. GRAY
143 West Overlook Drive
Nashville, TN 18755

May 22, 1997

Ms. Christine L. Volitip
Director of Corporate Planning
Johnson & Johnson
1 Johnson & Johnson Plaza
New Brunswick, NJ 18372

Dear Ms. Volitip:

Do you have need for an employee who can provide management with timely information on which crucial decisions (e.g., marketing of company products, the opening of new branches, diversification of company operations, examination of the effects of new tax laws, preparation of economic forecasts, etc.) are made?

I hold an M.S. degree in Economics and Operations Research and am seeking a position with a growing organization that can fully challenge my research capabilities in pursuit of the firm's objectives.

The enclosed resume reflects solid achievement in both the classroom and during my brief professional career. Whether in the classroom or at the workplace, I have been consistently able to meet near-term objectives while developing the tools to successfully tackle future requirements.

Thank you for your time. I look forward to hearing from you. References will be furnished upon request.

Sincerely,

Tyler W. Gray

Tyler W. Gray

TWG/acr

Enclosure

RICHARD R. REARDON

605 East Caroline Street   Home: (303) 875-0924
West Bradford, NH 177235   Office:(303) 977-0525

August 31, 1994

Ms. Nancy A. Anderson
Director of MIS
Vector Analytics, Inc.
127 East Bay Avenue
Boston, MA 17395

Dear Ms. Anderson:

I am seeking a position in data processing management and have enclosed my resume
for review against your current requirements.

My background in data processing includes programming, systems analysis, project
management, data base administration and MIS department management.

For the past seven years, I have been the Information Center Manager at Wilson
Corporation in Gorham, New Hampshire, responsible for planning, budgeting,
organizing and managing the daily operations of this department. In addition to
supporting all end user computing on the IBM 3090 mainframe and personal
computers, I am also responsible for evaluating PC hardware and software,
establishing PC standards and policies, consulting in the design of PC
applications and maintaining both mainframe and PC security controls.

I am seeking a position in the $65,000 to $70,000 range and have no relocation
restrictions.

Should you have an appropriate opening in your operations, I would appreciate the
opportunity to meet with you and the members of your staff to see how my
qualifications might align with your requirements. Thank you for your
consideration, and I look forward to hearing from you shortly.

Very truly yours,

Richard R. Reardon

Richard R. Reardon

RRR/cag

Enclosure

MITCHELL W. HARDY
133 Grand Banks Avenue
Annapolis, MD 19463
(301) 972-5125

June 15, 1993

Mr. Harold T. Wilston
Vice President of Marketing
Eastman Kodak Company
Eastman Plaza
Rochester, NY 17223

Dear Mr. Wilston:

In the course of attempting to revitalize and strengthen your company's sales and marketing strategy, you may have a requirement for an accomplished advertising executive.

Having been continually challenged and rapidly promoted, my career covers a variety of products and services, including packaged goods, insurance, technical/industrial businesses and corporate financial/image communications.

More specifically, I have:

> Developed the marketing analysis and implemented creative planning which led to improved sales for a mature, declining brand.

> In a similar role, helped maintain another brand's growth momentum with an imaginative advertising and promotion program for a line extension.

> In addition, I have strengthened and managed corporate advertising which helped change the ways senior business executives, consumers and the financial community perceived several major blue chip corporations.

While challenging marketing and customer communications problems are of primary importance to me, you should know that my total compensation requirements are in the $85,000 to $90,000 range.

May we talk?

Sincerely,

Mitchell W. Hardy

Mitchell W. Hardy

MWH/bar

Enclosure

BARBARA F. DAVIS
122 Hilltop Lane
Green Bay, WI 17228

February 12, 1998

Dorton T. Dixon
President
Vocar Corporation
166 West River Road
Pittsburgh, Pa 19826

Dear Mr. Dixon:

I am seeking an employment opportunity in an executive level sales, marketing or general management position that capitalizes on my capital goods and/or environmental background.

With over twenty years in industrial sales and marketing with the Square D Electric Company, refined with two corporate turnarounds and several start-up company assignments, I have been assisting high tech growth firms and troubled companies realize their profit potential.

My consulting practice has exposed me to the environmental services sector and given me the opportunity to start-up a hospital waste disposal business and underground storage tank & ground water remediation business. I have also assisted a petroleum distributor and contractor with an aggressive growth program and a reorganized major U.S. welding equipment manufacturer with a successful acquisition/merger.

While most of my successes have been in the marketing arena, I would welcome an opportunity in a division general management position that would capitalize on both my entrepreneurial and marketing strengths.

I will relocate with assistance, prefer the Northeast, and will leave compensation open to negotiation.

Sincerely,

Barbara F. Davis

Barbara F. Davis

BFD/dah

Enclosure

THORTON D. WILLIAMS
142 West Clairion Road
Sommersdell, NJ 19375
(609) 577-8796

May 14, 1998

Mr. Sears R. Dresher
President
Pardon Foods, Inc.
431 Union Street
Syracuse, NY 18662

Dear Mr. Dresher:

If you are seeking a top flight Chief Financial Officer, perhaps I may fit the bill.

In February of 1993, just after the market crash, I was successful in securing an investment grade rating on a $160 million debt for Munchies Food Systems, the first time in the company's history - this was accomplished without the Canadian parent's credit support. In 1995, I successfully refinanced $110 million of acquisition debt for a U.S. subsidiary of Walton Foods. It allowed them to sell the company for a premium.

During my tenure as senior or chief financial officer with past employers, I have developed several new credit facilities through both private and public sources. In some cases, these have been quite unique. For instance, the first insured, unleveraged multi-property real estate investment deal for the food franchising industry was masterminded by me. This business has grown to over $3.6 billion of assets now under management. I have employed captive lending facilities to improve investor returns as well as tax advantaged concepts like money market preferred stock. Of course, more traditional means like commercial paper and direct bank borrowing have been sourced as well.

I have one of those interesting business backgrounds with successful experience in manufacturing, distribution, financial services and retail. For nineteen years, cash flow improvement, whether through financing, cost containment/reduction, or revenue enhancement, has been a consistent result of my efforts in all of my business endeavors.

I have decided to seek a better opportunity. Although I am far more interested in an intriguing challenge and a good company then merely making money, you should know that in recent years my total compensation has been in the $140,000 to $160,000 range.

Should you be seeking a senior financial officer with my credentials, Mr. Dresher, I would very much appreciate the opportunity of meeting with you. Thank you for your consideration.

Sincerely,

Thorton D. Williams

Thorton D. Williams

MARY BETH WILLISON

800 Thornbush Way   Home: (616) 667-9178
Wellington, OR 28375   Office:(616) 887-9273

July 17, 1996

Mr. Robert Delrobia
Director of Procurement
Foster General Corporation
500 East Industry Highway, NE
Atlanta, GA 16284

Dear Mr. Delrobia:

I have six years of increasing responsibility as a Purchasing professional, including two years as a manager reporting to the Division Manager of Helgran Company's hair-care products business. A sampling of some of my key accomplishments includes:

- Saved $800,000 in raw materials costs in 10 months for an established brand through supplier contract re-negotiations

- Consolidated purchasing for polywrap and negotiated national contract producing over $1.2 million annual savings

- Installed JIT computer system cutting spare parts inventory requirements and saving $1/2 million annually in inventory investment

- Initiated changes in folding carton specification that increased packaging functionality and cut vital supplies inventory investment by $220,000 annually.

The enclosed resume will provide you with further particulars on contributions that I have made to my employer. Perhaps Foster General Corporation may wish to capitalize on my creativity and energy as well. If so, I can be reached at either my office or home telephone numbers listed above.

I hope that we will have the opportunity to discuss my qualifications further during a personal meeting. Thank you for your consideration.

Very truly yours,

Mary Beth Willison

Mary Beth Willison

MBW/vap

Enclosure

MICHAEL A. BAXTER
200 Ripple Drive
Deer Lake, IL 19284

September 15, 1995

Mr. John A Upton
Director of Employment
Farrel Paper Company, Inc.
1600 Stoney Creek Road
Neenah, WI 145915

Dear Mr. Upton:

I have been employed with the Carlton Paper Company for the last 3 years, and have decided to make a change. I am originally from the Appleton area, and would like the opportunity to return to Wisconsin.

I noted that Farrel Paper was undergoing considerable expansion, with plans to add three plants and a research center over the next 3 years. This suggests that you will be needing to recruit the technical and operations personnel to staff this major expansion. Perhaps I can be of help.

I hold a B.A. degree in Business from Western Michigan University and have 3 years of experience as Technical Employment Manager with Carlton Paper. As such, I have responsibility for all technical and operations staffing for the company, including the Technology Center and 6 manufacturing plants. During the last 2 years alone, I have recruited and successfully filled 150 technical and/or operations professional and managerial positions.

Some key accomplishments include:

- Staffed over 200 professional and managerial positions in 3
  years

- Reduced employee turnover by 30% through implementation of
  improved interviewing and selection techniques

- Reduced interview-to-hire ratio by 28%, saving over $50,000
  per year in candidate travel expenses

- Reduced recruiting time by 50% through implementation of
  creative recruiting strategies

If you will be needing an experienced employment professional who has first-hand knowledge of technical and operations recruiting in the paper industry, you may want to give me a call. I am sure that I can provide the kind of recruiting support that will be required by Farrel Paper to successfully meet its staffing requirements and achieve its expansion objectives.

Thank you for your consideration.

Sincerely,

Michael A. Baxter

Enclosure

SANDRA B. JACKSON

500 Melon Place
Lewisburg, PA 18224

Office: (717) 555-1234
Home: (717) 459-9821

February 16, 1998

Mr. Gordon D. Hammner
Vice President Marketing
Hillsboro Development Corporation
100 River Road
Milton, PA 19338

Dear Mr. Hammner:

I am seeking a challenging real estate business development sales and marketing position with an organization who can effectively use my knowledge and skills. My professional business career exhibits a record of strong achievement and significant contributions. The enclosed resume details my experience and accomplishments.

During my 4 years of highly successful business development and sales & marketing experience, I have been recognized for my creative spirit and ability to identify and implement profitable projects. The following highlights some of my career achievements:

- Arranged financing for acquisition and development costs and prepared all necessary proforma and cash flow analysis for a $6 million commercial development project

- Implemented successful sales and marketing plan to establish a strong presence for a Central Pennsylvania office of a Philadelphia-based development company

- Sold over $22 million in aggregate real estate leaseholds (56) during first 24 months (over 5 million square feet of commercial/industrial real estate)

- Obtained all necessary approvals for a 300 unit residential subdivision

If my qualifications of are interest to you, I would welcome the chance to meet with you personally and further explore career opportunities at Hillsboro Development Corporation. Thank you for considering my qualifications.

Sincerely,

Sandra B. Jackson

Sandra B. Jackson

Enclosure

DAVID P. WYNODD, PHD
135 Weston Place
Sandusky, Ohio 18239

February 14, 1994

Dr. Richard L. Longsdorf
Director Research & Development
Fowler Chemical Company
800 Commerce Drive
Cleveland, Ohio 17226

Dear Dr. Longsdorf:

I am seeking a challenging position in chemistry in the paints and coatings, chemical, petroleum, or rubber industry. My interests, education and experience qualify me particularly in the areas of product development, quality control, chemical safety and handling of hazardous substances.

My innovative and successful career has centered around formulation, characterization, and physical testing of polymer coatings, elastomers and fibers. My knowledge of many laboratory instruments, experience in customer service, public speaking, and technical presentations should prove valuable assets.

After you have reviewed my resume, I would appreciate the opportunity to discuss my credentials and how I might contribute to Fowler Chemical Company and its technical objectives.

Thank you.

Sincerely,

David P. Wynodd

David P. Wynodd

DPW/gal

Enclosure

SAMUEL T. SLATER

52 Tall Oak Lane, Framingham, MA 13429

April 28, 1997

Mr. William T Wentworth
Director of Marketing
Johnson Controls, Inc.
300 Commonwealth Avenue
Boston, MA 13489

Dear Mr. Wentworth:

Your review of my enclosed resume will be appreciated.

Briefly, I am a senior sales representative with broad
program management experience and a technical background
in process control and measurement as applied to production,
transmission, and distribution of electricity and various
industrial processes.

Should you have a suitable requirement that is appropriate
to my experience, please contact me by phone at (613) 975-
8873. I would be pleased to meet with you at your convenience.

Very truly yours,

Samuel T. Slater

Samuel T. Slater

Enclosure

ROBERT B. REDFIELD
102 Wren Lane
Warren, Ohio 17239
(216) 527-3847

April 23, 1995

Mr. Willard T. Waverly
Regional Sales Manager
Abbott Laboratories
200 East Executive Drive
Cleveland, Ohio 18238

Dear Mr. Waverly:

As the Regional Sales Manager for one of America's premiere pharmaceutical companies, I am sure you are always on the lookout for outstanding sales talent. Should you, or one of the other Abbott sales regions, currently be on the market for a proven sales leader with an excellent record of achievement, you may want to give me a call.

My qualifications include a B.A. in Marketing from Ohio State and 4 years in pharmaceutical sales with Wyeth Laboratories here in the Midwestern Region. Some highlights of my career include:

- Doubled territory sales volume in 4 years time ($2 to $4 million).

- Increased new accounts from 350 to over 700.

- Won annual regional sales contest 2 years in a row

My full resume is enclosed for your reference.

I feel that career growth opportunities at Wyeth are somewhat limited, and I have made a decision to seek a sales position with a more progressive company offering greater opportunity for upward mobility. Compensation requirements are in the $55,000 to $60,000 range plus company automobile.

If you feel my credentials are of interest, I would welcome a call and the opportunity to interview with your firm. I can normally be reached at my home during the evening after 7:00 PM.

Thank you for your consideration.

Sincerely,

Robert B. Redfield

Robert B. Redfield

BARBARA D. STANTON
605 Northwood Circle
St. Louis, MO 24649
(307) 995-6836

July 29, 1997

Mr. Frank Lawton
Director of Manufacturing
Corning Glass Works, Inc.
Corning Square
Corning, NY 14579

Dear Mr. Lawton:

I am interested in exploring career opportunities in operations management with the Corning Glass Works, and have therefore enclosed my resume for your reference. Should you be in the market for a young, results-oriented manufacturing manager for one of your plants, I would encourage you to consider my credentials.

A 1992 graduate of Syracuse University with a B.S. degree in Industrial Engineering, I have just over 5 years manufacturing experience in the glass industry with the Wooten Glass Company. During this time, I advanced from Shift Supervisor - Furnace Operations to Operations Manager of a 400 employee pharmaceutical glass manufacturing operation.

Some of my major contributions include:

- Successful installation and start-up of a $25 million glass manufacturing line (on time & under budget)

- Automated packaging department resulting in 30% reduction in labor costs ($4 million annual savings)

- Redesigned work assignments for finishing department and initiated skills training, resulting in 20% increase in department productivity

My strong contributions in manufacturing, coupled with solid knowledge of glass manufacturing operations, should make me an attractive candidate for an operations management assignment with your company. Should you agree, I would welcome the opportunity to meet with you further explore this possibility.

Thank you for considering my qualifications, and I look forward to hearing from you.

Sincerely,

Barbara D. Stanton

Barbara D. Stanton

Enclosure

WILLIAM J. DAVIS

816 Kimberly Lane, Split Lip, OK 43168

February 26, 1997

Mr. Richard T. Boone
Director of Logistics
Marathon Oil Company
20 Tower Place
Houston, TX 29485

Dear Mr. Boone:

As Director of Logistics for a major oil company, I'm sure you are keenly aware of the financial contributions that a skilled Distribution Manager can make to the corporate bottom line. It is for this reason you may wish to pay particular attention to my employment qualifications as highlighted on the enclosed resume.

My credentials include a B.A. degree in Business Administration from the University of Alabama and over 15 years experience in distribution and distribution management in the chemical process and petrochemical industry. I am currently Distribution Manager for the Lubes Division of Philipps Petroleum.

Selected accomplishments include:

- Implemented regional warehousing concept, consolidating 12 warehouses into 5 regional centers ($8 million annual savings).

- Automated 3 regional warehouses allowing for unitized handling of finished product and reducing product damage by 60% (annual savings of $2 million)

- Negotiated national truck fleet maintenance contract, reducing maintenance costs by 20% ($1.8 million annual savings).

I am seeking a senior position in distribution management at either the corporate or division level. Compensation requirements are in the $75,000 to $85,000 range.

Should you have an appropriate management opening, I would welcome the opportunity to meet with you personally to explore the contributions that I could make to your distribution operations.

Thank you for your review of my qualifications, and I look forward to your reply.

Sincerely,

William J. Davis

William J. Davis

Enclosure

KAREN S. DICKERSON

245 Clear View Road
Nashville, TN 57205

Home: (314) 227-3948
Office: (314) 326-9687

August 26, 1996

Mr. Winston H. Featherbone
Director of Engineering
Charles T. Main, Inc.
205 Old Church Square
Boston, MA 31832

Dear Mr. Featherbone:

Preliminary research of your company indicates that your firm is engaged in handling large scale engineering and start-up projects in the waste treatment field. In particular, I am quite interested in the work that you are doing in the area of site remediation. This is a field in which I have some strong expertise.

As the enclosed resume will demonstrate, I am a degreed engineer with some 10 years experience in project engineering management of large-scale site remediation projects. During the last 4 years, in fact, I have been Site Remediation Engineering Manager for the Roy F. Weston Company, and have directed some of Weston's largest projects for the Environmental Protection Agency.

I am thoroughly versed in all aspects of site remediation including both site evaluation and analysis as well as on-site management of the remediation process itself. I am also familiar with a wide range of remediation technologies including low and high-temperature thermal treatment systems.

In addition to my project management expertise, I am also considered a key resource to the marketing group in the sale of Weston engineering and consulting services in the site remediation area. I have played a key role in helping to land over $85 million in site remediation engineering projects in the last 2 years alone.

If you are in the market for a strong engineering manager to manage and grow your site remediation business, perhaps you might want to give me a call. I have the technical, marketing and managerial expertise necessary to profitably lead a major expansion of this segment of your business, and place you in a highly competitive position in this dynamic, fast-growing market.

Thank you for your consideration, and I look forward to hearing from you shortly.

Sincerely

Karen S. Dickerson

Enclosure

123 Greenery Lane
New Orleans, LA 58292

March 16, 1997

Ms. Martha E. Swanson
Creative Director
The Rober Agency, Inc.
805 Park Avenue
New York, NY 12485

Dear Ms. Swanson:

Creativity is the lifeblood of the advertising profession and is the core value that separates the elite agency from the mundane and boring. My clients have been anything but bored, and their advertising-driven sales revenue increases have generated more than a mild interest in what I have to offer.

Unfortunately, although my current employer enjoys a healthy cash flow generated by my creative contributions to the firm, the agency is a small family-owned operation and there appears to be little opportunity for career growth beyond my current position. This has forced me to consider other employment alternatives.

Please accept my resume in application for a management position on your creative department's staff. I am seeking the opportunity to manage a small group in the development of creative ideas for T.V. commercials and national print media advertising campaigns. Compensation requirements are in the $90,000 range.

My portfolio is replete with award-winning, sales-getting advertising campaigns for such major companies as Westinghouse, Procter & Gamble, Campbell Soup, Johnson & Johnson, and others. Through the use of my creative talents, my employer has both landed and expanded business with these key firms, with sales revenues of these firms now valued at approximately $150 million annually.

Perhaps we should meet to explore how I might put my creative energies to work for your agency. Should you agree, please contact me at my home number during week nights after 8:00 PM.

Thank you for your consideration.

Very truly yours,

Linda D. Baker

Linda D. Baker

Enclosure

LINDA D. CARTER

145 Pheasant Run   Home: (325) 235-3342
Round Lake, NJ 13249   Office: (325) 445-2354

_____

July 12, 1995

Mr. John G. Hargrove
Director of Procurement
Fairfield Fabrics, Inc.
134 Delaware River Road
Trenton, NJ 14326

Dear Mr. Hargrove:

Enclosed please find my resume as application for the position of Senior
Buyer with your firm. Review of my credentials will quickly confirm that I
am a skilled and hard-working procurement professional with a propensity
for continuous improvement and a real knack for returning profit to the
bottom line.

Some of my more noteworthy contributions include:

- Consolidated corporate-wide purchases of key chemical
  resulting in volume discount and $5 million annual
  savings.

- Initiated blanket order system with 5 hour guaranteed
  delivery of key packing materials, reducing raw
  material inventory by 74% and resulting in $1.6 million
  annual savings.

- Secured 10% price reduction in the purchase of all rayon
  fiber from major supplier (annual savings of $1.1
  million).

I feel comfident that I can bring similar cost savings to Fairfield Fabrics
as well.

My qualifications include a B.S. degree in Chemistry from the University of
Delaware and 6 years of highly successful raw materials and packaging
procurement for a well-known manufacturer of nonwoven fabrics. I have been
continuously recognized by my employer for outstanding performance and can
furnish excellent references upon request.

Should you have a need for a strong procurement professional, I would hope
that you would give me a call. Thank you for considering my credentials,
and I look forward to your reply.

                                        Sincerely,

                                        Linda D. Carter

                                        Linda D. Carter

Enclosure

MICHAEL T. PATTERSON
133 Rip Tide Lane
Avalon, NJ 13254
(609) 556-9075

September 23, 1996

Mr. Jarl K. Swanson
Manager of MIS
ICI Americas, Inc.
Concord Pike & N. Murphy Road
Wilmington, DL 13426

Dear Mr. Swanson:

I heard some rumors through some of my industry contacts that ICI Americas is considering installation of a computerized MRP system throughout its Specialty Projects Division. If you are looking for a project leader or senior systems analyst for this project, I would be an ideal candidate!

My credentials include a B.S. in Computer Science from Penn State University and 4 years of experience as a systems analyst with Carson Chemical, Inc. Carson, as you may be aware, is a $560 million manufacturer of specialty chemicals sold to the agricultural chemicals industry. Currently, I hold the position of Senior Systems Analyst.

Of particular interest should be the fact that I have spent the last 2 years as the lead systems analyst in the installation and successful start-up of a computerized MRP system at Carson. This project was highly successful, and was completed ahead of time and on budget.

The Vice President of Manufacturing has stated that this was the most successful system installation that he has ever witnessed at Carson. The start-up was practically flawless, and the transition from manual system to computer was accomplished without missing a beat. The success of this project resulted in my receipt of a $5,000 special bonus as recognition for my contribution as the lead systems analyst.

I am enclosing a copy of my resume so that you might become familiar with the specifics of my qualifications and experience.

Should you have an interest in pursuing my candidacy, I would be pleased to hear from you. I can be reached at my home most evenings between the hours of 7:30 and 10:00 PM.

Thank you for your consideration.

Sincerely,

Michael T. Patterson

Michael T. Patterson

Enclosure

3

Letters to Search Firms

Search firms and employment agencies are statistically known to be important sources for use in the job search. Surveys show that these firms account for some 10 to 15 percent of all professional and managerial jobs found by the job seeker. These studies also demonstrate that such organizations are the second most productive source, second only to networking (personal contact), as a means of finding employment. This is a fact that should not go unnoticed when you design your job-hunting campaign.

In planning your job search, therefore, you will want to target search firms and/or employment agencies as a key source of jobs. Since most of these firms will not accept unsolicited telephone calls from job seekers, it is impractical to think of maximizing the use of this important job source by using the telephone or by simply "walking in the door" unexpectedly. This leaves only one practical means for accessing these firms—use of a direct-mail campaign.

Our firm, Brandywine Consulting Group, has experimented with the use of direct mail to search firms and employment agencies as a job search method. To date, results have shown that between 3 to 5 percent of those firms targeted will respond with an interest in the candidate. These statistics seem to hold true for professional through upper middle management level positions. There is, however, a significant drop-off in response rate for persons in very senior level executive positions (those at the top 5 percent of executive earnings levels).

This means that, if you are at the professional through upper-middle management level, it is probably well worth your while to use a mass mail approach in contacting these firms. In fact, even senior level executives will want to use this technique. However, executives at these senior levels should not have unrealistic expectations concerning the number of positive responses they will receive. A sizable mailing to 500 or 600 search firms/employment agencies should generally be expected to yield 15 to 30 favorable responses. By this, I mean that between

15 to 30 of the firms targeted through the mailing will likely call you to discuss a particular employment opening with one of their client companies.

In one relatively recent Brandywine Consulting Group mailing to some 800 companies, for example, the candidate for whom we made the mailing had approximately 24 such calls. These calls resulted in some 7 or 8 interviews and 3 job offers, one of which the candidate accepted. All of this activity occurred within 37 work days from initiation of this individual's job-hunting campaign.

So, this example clearly demonstrates that the direct-mail campaign, aimed at search firms and employment agencies, can prove to be a very powerful job search technique. A good broadcast cover letter can help facilitate the effectiveness of this job-hunting method.

PURPOSE OF COVER LETTER

The type of broadcast cover letter employed in making a mass mailing to search firms is somewhat different from that used to make a similar mailing to employers. This has to do with the differences in the roles of these two organizations.

The motivation of the employer is to find uniquely qualified individuals who can "add value" to their organization. As a result, it is believed that the employer will read the cover letter more thoroughly than the search firm or employment agency. They will generally look more broadly at the candidate's overall qualifications.

By contrast, the search firm or employment agency's role is that of matching the candidate's qualifications with the specifics of the employer's requirements. Thus, the role of these third parties is more focused on "matching" the qualifications of the candidate with the specific requirements contained in the employer's "candidate specification", rather than on looking at the candidate's broader credentials from a "value-adding" perspective. It is believed, therefore, that most third parties will frequently skip the cover letter and go right to the resume to facilitate this qualifications comparison.

Additionally, search firms and employment agencies, due to the volume of cover letters and resumes they receive, have long ago come to realize that the cover letter is frequently redundant to the resume, and contains much of the same information. Why, then, waste time reading the cover letter until you have established that an appropriate match exists through comparison of the candidate's resume and the client's candidate specification?

It is believed, therefore, that these firms view the cover letter principally as a "letter of transmittal." This is to say that they view the primary purpose of the cover letter as simply a vehicle for transmitting the candidate's resume, as opposed to a document that adds any real value to the selection/comparison process.

This is not to say that these firms won't take the time to read the cover letter. Most, in fact, do—but only after having established that there is an appropriate fit with their client's needs. There is, thus, much less likelihood that the candidate can effectively use the cover letter to "sell" the search firm or agency on his or her value. This, however, is not the case with the cover letter sent directly to employers. It is believed that these cover letters are better read by the employer, increasing the probability that the candidate might be invited in for an interview (or exploratory interview) based upon key factors contained in the cover letter.

KEY LETTER ELEMENTS

Since the purpose of the cover letter used with search firms and agencies is principally that of "resume transmittal", these letters tend to be relatively brief when compared to the broadcast letters sent directly to the employer. The principal difference between the two is that the search firm/employment agency letter places less emphasis on selling specific value and more emphasis on providing a general, overall summary of qualifications.

The following are key elements normally found in the search firm/employment agency broadcast cover letter:

1. First paragraph normally contains the following:
    a. Statement of job search objective (position sought)
    b. Request to be considered for firm's current and future job search assignments
2. Second paragraph normally contains an overall "qualifications summary" including:
    a. Educational credentials
    b. Relevant work experience
3. Third paragraph normally contains a "statement of appreciation" for the firm's review and consideration of your qualifications.

In addition to using the above "standard" paragraphs, authors of these types of cover letters may choose to include one or more of the following optional paragraphs:

1. Explanation of reason for making career change
2. A "selling" or "value-adding" paragraph citing key accomplishments relevant to job search objective
3. Statement specifying compensation requirements
4. Statement specifying geographical preferences or restrictions
5. Statement providing contact instructions

The balance of this chapter provides a wide selection of well-written search firm cover letters that should facilitate your design of an effective letter for use in your job-hunting campaign.

VICTORIA E. JOHNSON

829 Lindermere Lane, Green Valley, IN 13787

June 18, 1997

Mr. Ernest G. Haskins
The Goddard Agency
1345 West Beverly Blvd.
Cleveland, Ohio 16483

Dear Mr. Haskins:

I understand from some of my associates that your agency specializes in placing technical personnel in the electronics field. Perhaps you are currently working on an assignment for one of your clients which might align well with my qualifications and requirements.

I am seeking a position as a Programmer Analyst providing technical programming support to Development Engineers in the development of state-of-the-art communications controllers or related technology.

Key qualifications include:

- M.S. degree in Computer Science

- 3 years technical programming support experience in an R&D electronics environment

- In-depth knowledge of the SNA/ACP/NCP functions of a communications controller in a PEP environment

- Proficiency in SNA/ACP/NCP internals

- Proficiency with SDLC, various trace facilities, ALC and TSO/WYLBUR/SPF

- Expert in use of data analyzer equipment

My current annual compensation is $58,000, and I have no geographical restrictions.

Should you be aware of a suitable opportunity, I would appreciate hearing from you. Thank you for your consideration.

Sincerely,

Victoria E. Johnson

Victoria E. Johnson

VEJ/sam

Enclosure

JOHN R. THOMPSON
135 North Beaver Road
Sunny Creek, CA 15374

March 30, 1995

Mr. Norman L. Lindgren
Lindgren & Smith Associates
925 Tower Hill Road
San Francisco, CA 18475

Dear Mr. Lindgren:

Could one of your client companies use an ambitious, young accounting professional with an excellent record of growth and accomplishment as an accounting supervisor?

I am thoroughly trained and ready for my first supervisory assignment. I have a solid technical foundation in accounting fundamentals, which I have gained during my last 3 years of employment at Minute Man Electronics, Inc.. In addition, I have strong interpersonal, communications and leadership skills, which should serve me well in a supervisory role.

Beyond my professional experience, I hold both a B.A. and M.B.A. from Syracuse University, where I majored in accounting. As my resume will attest, I was both a scholar and a campus leader.

Although I would prefer to remain on the West Coast, I will give serious consideration to other locations, should the opportunity be a good one.

Should you identify a suitable opportunity for me, Mr. Lindgren, I can be reached on a confidential basis at my office during the day or at my home during evening hours. Both phone numbers are on the enclosed resume.

Thank you.

Sincerely,

John R. Thompson

John R. Thompson

Enclosure

R. WILSON PETERSON

200 Woodbine Road
Tampa, FL 13472

Home: (312) 557-0973
Office: (312) 957-0782

July 22, 1996

Mr. Willard B. Harrison
Senior Partner
Harrison & Bane, Inc.
200 Park Avenue
New York, NY 17263

Dear Mr. Harrison:

For the past several years I have been running the Chemicals Business for General Industries, Inc. In late 1995, that business was sold to Dow Chemical Company.

I am now in the process of a career change.

I understand that your company services the chemical industry and thought I would forward a copy of my resume for your information and review.

If you know of any opportunities, I would appreciate being considered.

If you need additional information or would like to discuss my qualifications in more detail, please give me a call.

Thank you in advance for your time and consideration.

Sincerely,

R. Wilson Peterson

RWP/mm

Enclosure

LINDA W. GARRISON
233 Day Street, SW
New Orleans, LA 19384
(205) 572-9472

October 10, 1994

Mr. Stephen R. Darby
The Darby Group
813 Cobble Creek Parkway
Dallas, TX 13948

Dear Mr. Darby:

I am seeking a project engineering position in the metals industry. My research indicates that your firm services clients in the metals and related industries, so I am enclosing my resume for your review and consideration.

I am an ambitious, young Senior Project Engineer with five years experience in the design, installation and start-up of aluminum manufacturing processes and equipment. I have strong engineering skills and have earned an excellent reputation for project timeliness and cost efficiency. The following are some of my key accomplishments:

- Managed mechanical design of $20 million aluminum furnace
  complex (completed on time and under budget).

- Redesigned refractory lining in a flash calciner process to
  reduce heat loss by 30% in existing and 50% in new units.
  (Potential savings $4.5 million annually).

- Directed design and installation of $12 million furnace and
  associated material handling equipment. (Completed 2 months
  ahead of schedule and 15% under budget).

Should one of your client companies be in search of a results-oriented, highly motivated senior project engineer with my credentials, I would appreciate the opportunity to further discuss my qualifications with you.

My geographical preference is the Southwestern United States, and my compensation requirements are in the low $70,000 range.

Thank you for your consideration, and I look forward to hearing from you.

Very truly yours,

Linda W. Garrison

Linda W. Garrisson

LWG/naf

Enclosure

WILLIAM B. CARSON

206 Summit Street
Asheville, NC 13487

Home: (216) 547–9572
Office: (216) 837–8372

September 14, 1993

Ms. Katherine B. Baxter
President
The Baxter Group, Inc.
305 Peachtree Street, NW
Atlanta, GA 19385

Dear Ms. Baxter:

I am taking this opportunity to write to you regarding career opportunities that may exist within your client community.

My current position is Director of Systems Development with Computer World Stores in Asheville, North Carolina, and I was previously with the Information Services Division of Carter Hawley Hale Stores in Anaheim, California.

I have in excess of 20 years of experience in retail systems development within the MIS organizations, which includes major accomplishments in systems development, data administration, data center computer operations, information center and quality assurance departments.

Although I'm far more interested in finding a good company and an interesting opportunity, you will want to be aware that my annual compensation has been in the $125,000 to $130,000 range during the last few years.

I look forward to having the opportunity to more fully describe my qualifications, should you have a suitable assignment for which you wish to consider me. Thank you.

Sincerely,

William B. Carson

William B. Carson

WBC/say

Enclosure

JOSEPH W. WALTERS

402 North Canyon Road, Billsly, OK 18274   (604) 977-2849

May 13, 1996

Mr. David P. Grace
Grace and Foster, Inc.
Suite 800 Tower Place
1600 Commerce Blvd, SW
Houston, TX 15839

Dear Mr. Grace:

I am writing to you in hopes that you are currently providing service to client firms seeking uniquely talented claims management or operations professionals for the insurance industry. With a consistent track record of success within both the property & casualty and managed healthcare industries, I believe that I could contribute immediately to a variety of claims and operational issues.

I have enclosed my resume to provide you with the details of my background and skills. I would be most anxious to discuss my career goals with you - even if on a purely exploratory basis.

If you have any immediate questions, do not hesitate to call. Should you have employment opportunities which you feel may be of interest to me, I would appreciate hearing from you. My phone number is (604) 977-2849.

Thank you for your consideration, and I look forward to hearing from you.

Sincerely,

Joseph W. Walters

Joseph W. Walters

JWW/wap

Enclosure

DAWN M. MARKS
106 Summit Avenue
Shillington, PA 19317
(215) 775-2184

March 14, 1996

Ms. Carline T. Barsdale
President
Barsdale, Sloan & Associates
Suite 202 Liberty Place
1600 Market Street
Philadelphia, PA 19113

Dear Ms. Barsdale:

Enclosed please find my resume for your review and consideration against either current or future search assignments in the field of Human Resources.

I am seeking a responsible and challenging corporate or division level position as a human resource generalist. Consideration would also be given to a position in the field of Labor Relations.

My salary requirements are in the $75K+ range with flexibility dependent upon area, future opportunity and other similar factors. Although I have no absolute geographical restrictions, I do have a strong preference for the North and Southeast areas.

Thank you for your consideration, and I look forward to the prospect of discussing appropriate career opportunities with you or a member of your staff.

Sincerely,

Dawn M. Marks

DMM/art

Enclosure

CHRISTOPHER T. BEATTY

818 Kimberly Lane
West Chester, PA 19382

Home: (215) 430-1474
Office: (215) 577-0987

May 24, 1996

Mr. Carlton C. Biggins
Senior Partner
Biggins, Smathers & Johnson
Suite # 120
Waterview Towers
300 East Bay Avenue
Seattle, WA 15274

Dear Mr. Biggins:

I am seeking challenging opportunities in Operations Management at the corporate, division, or major operating facility level. Perhaps one of your current or future clients may be looking for a strong Operations Executive and have an interest in my qualifications.

As my resume shows, I have had excellent career progression in the field of Operations Management at both DuPont and Dow Chemical Company. Unfortunately, the division for which I have been working has been sold and my position as Director of Operations eliminated.

You will note from my resume that I have established an excellent track record for generating overall cost reduction and operation efficiency improvements for each of my past employers. I take particular pride in staying current with new approaches and methodologies for improving operations, and am quick to apply those that will generate solid bottom line results.

If one of your clients seeks a highly-motivated Operations Executive with strong leadership skills and a demonstrated record for running efficient and profitable operations, perhaps you will think of me.

I can be reached, during the day or evening, at the numbers listed on the letterhead.

Very truly yours,

Christopher T. Beatty

CTB/rhb

Enclosure

TRACY M. VANDIVERE

206 Winding Lane
Colombia, MD 19384

Home: (305) 283-1928
Office: (305) 773-0928

May 16, 1976

Mr. Roger G. Borabach
Senior Partner
Search International, Inc.
3005 Market Street
Philadelphia, PA 19837

Dear Mr. Borabach:

I am a results-oriented, senior level marketing executive with over fourteen years experience in all phases of marketing and sales management. Innovativeness has proven to be my greatest asset, and I am credited with substantial increases in overall sales volume for each of my past employers as a result of the fresh new market approaches and creative ideas that I have contributed to these organizations.

The following are some of my key accomplishments:

- Catapulted Company to Number 1 in sales in European specialty resins market in only 2 years (33% increase in export sales)

- Led national roll-out of new low viscosity resin product with resultant $85 million sales in first year

- Repositioned old brand through creative advertising approach that revitalized product and resulted in 150% increase in sales volume in 6 months.

- Replaced independent manufacturers representative network with direct salesforce, reducing cost-of-sales 30% over 3 year period.

- Directed installation of order tracking computer system that led to reduction in order delivery time of 23% in 18 months.

My enclosed resume further details my extensive experience and qualifications as a marketing executive.

Should one of your specialty chemicals clients be in the market for a top-flight marketing and sales executive as a member of their senior management team, perhaps you will give my qualifications serious consideration. My marketing knowledge, creativity and energy could prove a valuable asset in helping them to realize their full growth potential.

Thank you for your time and consideration.

Sincerely,

Tracy M. Vandivere

Enclosure

126 Sunnyside Road
Mobile, AL 18273

July 5, 1996

Ms. Cheryl L. Mannington
President
The Mannington Consulting Group
800 Trade Center Avenue
Birmingham, AL 18274

Dear Ms. Mannington:

I am a senior human resources executive with over fifteen years experience. Currently, I am Director of Corporate Staff Human Resources for Scott Paper Company, a $5.5 billion, Fortune 200, consumer products company.

Although Scott has generally been good to me, I have some concerns about future career progression due to a long-term strategy designed to reduce the size of the corporate staff organization. This consolidation, coupled with the relatively young age of the top human resource executives, suggests that future career progression at the senior levels will be severely limited in the short to intermediate term. I have thus opted to confidentially explore other career options outside of the company.

My qualifications include an M.B.A. from Michigan State University with an emphasis in Human Resource Management. My career progression at Scott has included human resource management assignments at the corporate, division and manufacturing plant level. I am well schooled and heavily seasoned in a wide range of human resource functions including: organization design, management development, employment, compensation and benefits, and labor relations.

I am seeking a senior human resources position at the vice presidential level, with full responsibility for all human resource functions. Compensation requirements are in the six figure range, and I am open to relocation to most parts of the U.S.

Should one of your clients be in the market for a senior level human resources executive with my credentials, I would appreciate a call. Thank you for your consideration.

Sincerely,

Jeffrey A. Morse

Enclosure

BARRY D. SANDERS, Ph.D
14 Wellsley Court
Akron, Ohio 16238
(216) 375-0941

January 13, 1994

Mr. Harold F. Haupt
Senior Consultant
Technical Placement, Inc.
100 East Surrey Road
Columbus, Ohio 16283

Dear Mr. Haupt:

I am a **Ph.D organic chemist** from Princeton University with twelve years of experience in R&D and R&D management, and also hold an **MBA** with three years experience in **business development and analysis** including acquisitions, foreign joint ventures and strategic planning.

My areas of technical expertise are polymer **composites**, **adhesives**, polymer chemistry in **unsaturated polyester, vinyl ester, urethane** and **epoxy, fine organic chemicals, petrochemicals**, and homogeneous and heterogeneous **catalysis**.

I am capable of handling a wide spectrum of business development projects ranging from new application/product development and new market development, to creating entirely new businesses, to strategic expansion via acquisition and joint venture.

I am seeking a **management** position in a technology-oriented polymer chemical company in **business/market development** or **research and development**, where I can fully utilize both my technical and business expertise to create new business opportunities for my employer.

I am willing to relocate, and would consider positions paying in excess of $80,000 per year.

If you are aware of a suitable employment opportunity with one of your clients, I would appreciate hearing from you. Thank you.

Yours very truly,

Barry D. Sanders

Barry D. Sanders

Enclosure

WANDA MADDRE-RANDOLPH

202 Roosevelt Drive　　　　　　　　　　　　　　　　　**Home: (314) 773-2323**
Newark, DL 19873　　　　　　　　　　　　　　　　　　**Office: (314) 665-1927**

April 26, 1995

Mr. Richard H. Pepperman
Pepperman Sheets & Company
220 Landers Avenue
Allentown, PA 19372

Dear Mr. Pepperman:

Your clients may be in search of a Total Quality Manager, who has successfully led the implementation of an SPC-based total quality effort on a company-wide basis. I have successfully led such an effort. Enclosed is my resume which provides specifics of my qualifications.

OBJECTIVE	-- Corporate Manager - Total Quality
LOCATION	-- Northeastern United States
COMPENSATION	-- $70,000 to $75,0000 Range
TRAVEL	-- Up to 60% Acceptable

Should you require further information, I can be reached at the phone numbers listed in the letterhead.

Thank you.

Sincerely,

Wanda Maddrey-Randolph

Wanda Maddrey-Randolph

Enclosure

SCOTT M. BRANFORD

401 Valley Parkway, Wayne, PA 19837   (413) 997-8152

April 23, 1994

Ms. Della T. James
The Cheshire Group
200 Raintree Avenue
Malvern PA 19284

Dear Ms. James:

Although I enjoy the challenges of my present position, I am seeking alternatives to a lengthy commute into New York City. You may have a requirement for a procurement professional with strong background in purchasing of packaging materials.

I am now Buyer - Packaging Materials for the Wharton Paper Company, a $1.6 billion manufacturer of consumer paper products and sanitary tissues. As such, I purchase over $30 million of packaging materials and vital supplies annually. This includes, polywrap, folding cartons, and corrugated containers for the company's 4 manufacturing plants.

Enclosed is a current resume for your records. Although salary is not my first consideration, my minimum compensation requirement is $55,000.

Should my qualifications be a match for one of your needs, I would appreciate hearing from you. Thank you for your consideration.

Sincerely,

Scott M. Branford

Scott M. Branford

SMB/tap

Enclosure

435 East Michigan Avenue
Washington, DC 16283

August 12, 1996

Ms. Joan A. Higby
Sales Professionals, Inc.
200 West Maryland Avenue
Washington, DC 16284

Dear Ms. Higby:

I am an accomplished sales professional with four years experience in selling complex business systems to a variety of business applications. My enclosed resume will detail the specifics of my experience and accomplishments, however, I would like to highlight the fact that I have been the top regional Sales Representative for the Eastern Region for the last 3 years running.

I am seeking a senior sales or district sales management position selling "big ticket" business systems (i.e., computers, mailing systems, microfilm systems, etc.) to governmental agencies, manufacturing, and/or services businesses. I particularly enjoy selling complex systems that require applications problem solving for marketing success. This is an area of particular strength for me, and one which I find very satisfying.

Briefly, my qualifications include a B.S. degree in Psychology from the University of Maryland and four years selling microfilm systems for the Berry Corporation. During this period, I have increased sales in my territory by 150% and have replaced competition at several major accounts. Major customers include: the U.S. Department of Labor, the U.S. Department of the Navy, DuPont, IBM, General Dynamics and Black & Decker - to mention a few.

If any of your client companies are looking for an accomplished sales professional with strong background in business equipment systems sales, I would welcome the opportunity to talk with them. Compensation requirements are in the $80,000 range, and I am open to relocation to most areas of the country.

Thank you for your review of my qualifications, and I hope to hear from you shortly.

Sincerely,

Donald K. Bassett

Donald K. Bassett

DKB/rem

Enclosure

JARL R. SWANSON
336 Westerlies Lane
Norfolk, VA 13948

March 15, 1995

Brentwood Consulting Group
102 Brigade Avenue
Valley Forge, PA 19374

Dear Sir/Madam:

This summer I will be completing my obligation as an officer in the United States Navy, and will be making the transition to civilian employment. A complete resume detailing my qualifications is enclosed for your reference.

The following highlights my job search objectives:

EMPLOYMENT OBJECTIVE: Engineering or engineering project management position

PREFERRED LOCATION: Greater Philadelphia area (Open to other geographical locations)

TRAVEL AVAILABILITY: Up to 50% travel is acceptable

SALARY REQUIREMENTS: Flexible -- $60,000 minimum

AVAILABILITY: Late July, 1995

If you are aware of any positions with your client companies that would allow me to utilize and refine my engineering and/or engineering management skills, please call. I look forward to hearing from you.

Thank you.

Sincerely,

Jarl R. Swanson

Jarl R. Swanson

Enclosure

ARTHUR P. WAINSCOTT

122 Wild Duck Lane
Heavenly, NC 15249

Home: (917) 874-0434
Office: (917) 773-9092

June 1, 1994

Mr. Daniel P Warbuck
Senior Principal
Warbuck & Smathers, Inc.
800 Cross Creek Parkway
Atlanta, GA 18374

Dear Mr. Warbuck:

I am writing to inquire of possible positions with any of your clients as a General Manager or Plant Manager in the chemical or related industries.

As Plant Manager for a large chemical company, I brought the operation from a $12 million loss to a $7 million profit in only seven years. I used TQM methods to achieve significant cost reductions and productivity improvements, via personnel training and development. A strong customer orientation and business team interaction created good market penetration through an improved level of service and customer-focused product enhancements.

As the enclosed resume shows, I have over 15 years of extensive, diversified experience in the chemical industry. I would like to bring my proven track record for cost reduction and product development to an entrepreneurial, growing organization that can benefit from my knowledge and experience.

As a follow-up to this correspondence, I will plan to call you to determine what, if any, opportunities may exist with your clients. If no appropriate opportunities exist, I would welcome your ideas and counsel.

Thank you for your time, and I look forward to talking with you shortly.

Sincerely,

Arthur P. Wainscott

Arthur P Wainscott

APW/clm

Enclosure

VIRGINIA HALLETT HIRONS

200 Tall Palms Blvd., Tampa, FL 17294   (317) 284-1726

June 20, 1994

Mr. Scott M. Beatty
President
The Beatty Group, Inc.
102 Market Street
West Chester, PA 19382

Dear Mr. Beatty:

I am a graduate of the Wharton School with an MBA in Finance and 3 years experience as a Financial Analyst with the Harris Aerospace Corporation here in Tampa. I have decided to make a career change and am interested in finding a similar position with a company in the consumer products industry. Perhaps one of your clients may have an interest in my background.

The following have been some key accomplishments at Harris:

- Developed manufacturing cost projections and funding requirements for a $200 million missile guidance project

- Secured funding for $500 million business expansion at highly favorable terms

- Developed computer model for projection of manufacturing costs for new electronic subassemblies

- Recipient of 2 government commendations for outstanding achievement in financial planning

I am young and ambitious, and will have an interest only in those companies who can demonstrate clear opportunities for rapid career advancement based upon knowledge and contribution to the business. Opportunities for advancement into management short-term will also be a factor in my decision.

I would prefer positions in the Northeast, with a particular interest in the Philadelphia area. I am open to other locations, however, dependent upon the specifics of the opportunity. Compensation requirements are in the $70,000 range.

I would hope to hear from you shortly, should you have an appropriate opportunity which you feel may be of interest to me. Thank you for your consideration.

Sincerely,

Hallett Hirons

V. Hallett Hirons

Enclosure

BRADFORD S. RAWLINS
825 North Hill Road
Portland, OR 14279

February 18, 1996

The Wilshire Group
800 High Top Hill
San Francisco, CA 18274

Dear Sir/Madam:

I am an experience Accounting Executive seeking an opportunity for further career advancement in accounting/financial management.

Some of my accomplishments are outlined in the enclosed resume.

My ability to creatively deal with rapid growth and to manage and develop people, in addition to technical qualifications, are well documented and should allow me to make a significant contribution to the right company.

I have no geographical restrictions. Salary requirements are negotiable as appropriate with the specific opportunity.

Since my current employer is unaware of my decision to seek other employment, I would appreciate your treating this inquiry with appropriate sensitivity. I can be reached discreetly at work at (217) 887-9024 or through my wife at home at (217) 667-9992.

Thank you for your consideration.

Sincerely

Bradford S. Rawlins

Bradford S. Rawlins

BSR/dal

Enclosure

JOEL T. GOLDBERG
204 East Wyncott Drive
Flint, Michigan 19284

June 11, 1994

Ms. Laura T. Jenkins
The Bradford Group, Inc.
200 E. Michigan Avenue
Detroit, MI 19282

Dear Ms. Jenkins:

Enclosed please find my resume.

I possess a significant record of accomplishment in Senior level Marketing/Sales Management positions along with early exposure to Accounting and Finance. My experience has been gained in diverse situations ranging from new ventures, business development/acquisitions, to two highly successful turnarounds.

My objective is to continue progression in the Marketing/Sales Management field or to pursue an opportunity in General Management.

I would appreciate being considered for any opportunity you deem appropriate.

Thank you in advance for your consideration. I look forward to speaking with you in the near future.

Sincerely,

Joel T. Goldberg

Joel T. Goldberg

JTG/hcg

Enclosure

STEPHEN C. TEMPLE

818 General Howe Drive   Home: (215) 431-1726
Chadds Ford, PA 19382   Office: (215) 696-0821

July 16, 1996

Mr. John Kelleter
Kelleter & Sweeney Associates
100 North Blvd.
Miami, FL 16284

Dear Mr. Kelleter:

It has come to my attention that your firm specializes in executive search consulting in the field of Human Resources. Since I am a specialist seeking a senior level position in Employment, it seems appropriate to forward my resume for your review against current search assignments.

As you can see from my resume, I hold an M.S. in Psychology from the University of Michigan and have over 14 years experience in the field of Human Resources, with nearly 10 years in Employment. I am currently Director of Employment for Beecham Laboratories, a $1.5 billion manufacturer of proprietary pharmaceuticals. In this capacity I manage a staff of 5 professionals and provide corporate-wide recruiting and internal staffing support to a 5 plant, 22,000 employee organization.

My wife, Peggy, has just completed her MBA in Finance at the Wharton School and has received an excellent employment offer from Ford Aerospace in Orlando. We both enjoy sailing and have always been attracted to the Florida area. This offers the perfect opportunity for us to make a move.

Please consider my credentials for any employment-related search assignments you are currently conducting for firms located in the Orlando or surrounding areas (up to 1-1/2 hours commute). Although I would prefer an assignment at the Director level, I realize that I may need to be flexible in order to realize my geographical objective. Minimum compensation requirements are in the mid $60,000 range.

Thank you for taking the time to review my credentials, and I look forward to hearing from you.

Sincerely,

Stephen C. Temple

Stephen C. Temple

SCT/pmt

Enclosure

MARGARET R. TEMPLE
818 General Howe Drive
Chadds Ford, PA 19382

January 3, 1996

Ms. Regina Kelleter
Kelleter & Sweeney Associates
100 North Blvd.
Miami, FL 16284

Dear Ms. Kelleter:

I will be receiving an MBA in Finance from the Wharton School in June of this year, and am seeking a position as a Financial Analyst with a high-technology manufacturing or research company in Florida or one of the Southern Coastal States. My husband, Steve, and I are avid sailors and our objective is to be near a large body of water.

Besides graduating with honors in Finance, highlights of my qualifications include 2 years of employment as a Contract Cost Accountant with Belvar Electronics, Inc. and 2 summers of employment in the Corporate Finance Department of General Electric's Aerospace Division in Valley Forge, Pennsylvania. While at GE, I handled financial projections for several classified electronics projects.

Compensation requirements are in the high $60,000 range.

Should you be aware of a suitable opportunity with one of your clients, I would appreciate hearing from you.

Thank you for your consideration.

Sincerely,

Margaret R. Temple

Margaret R. Temple

Enclosure

CAROLYN A. BEATTY

818 Kimberly Lane   Home: (215) 431-7414
Chadds Ford, PA 19382   Office: (215) 622-5125

May 16, 1996

Mr. John M. Dresher
The Dresher Group
525 Park Avenue
New York, NY 17364

Dear Mr. Dresher:

I am an experienced Architectural Engineer with over 10 years experience in architectural design of commercial high-rise structures. Most recently, I was the Lead Engineer in the design of Liberty Place, the 62 story commercial high-rise building that now dominates the Philadelphia skyline and has won numerous national design awards.

Other major projects with which I have played a key design role include the Baltimore Aquarium, Skyline Towers (a 32 story office building in Baltimore), and Surrey Place West (a 22 story office complex in Washington, D.C.). In my 10-1/2 years in the Architectural Design field, I have won over 20 national and local awards for design excellence.

Unfortunately, Ronnan Associates, Inc., the major development firm with which I have been associated since the beginning of my career, has just filed for Chapter Eleven bankruptcy, and a massive reorganization of the company is now under way. It seems appropriate at this time for me to think about moving on with my career.

I am seeking a senior engineering or management position with a major developer or architectural engineering firm specializing in the design and/or construction of commercial high-rise structures. Compensation requirements are in the six figure range, and I would prefer an equity position in the firm, if available.

Relocation is no obstacle. I am quite willing to go where the opportunity is, however, I do have a preference for the Northeast. Overseas assignments will also be considered.

Should one of your clients have an appropriate position which you feel may be of interest to me, I would appreciate a call. Thank you for your consideration.

Sincerely,

Carolyn A. Beatty

Carolyn A. Beatty

Enclosure

208 High Street
West Chester, PA 19382

April 15, 1997

Mr. Landon M. Spilman
Spilman & Myers Associates
200 Valley View Parkway
Malvern, PA 19284

Dear Mr. Spilman:

I was informed by a colleague that your firm has some specialization in the placement of Materials and Logistics professionals. I am thus enclosing my resume for your consideration in light of assignments you may be working on that require someone with my credentials.

As my resume shows, I have a B.S. in Business Administration from Lafayette College and three years experience in Procurement with the Davis Pharmaceutical Company here in Philadelphia. Some of my key accomplishments while at Davis are as follow:

- Saved $1.3 million through negotiation of 2 year contract on knock-down cartons at a price 20% below past pricing level

- Used computer analysis to adjust order cycle on polywrap, reducing inventory by 36% ($3/4 million savings annually)

- Selected, modified and installed raw material forecasting computer system allowing greater control and efficiency in accurately forecasting and planning raw materials and supplies inventory requirements

Davis Pharmaceutical, as you may be aware, has recently been acquired by Galaxo, a London-based pharmaceutical giant. Galaxo has announced plans to cut back on the management staff at Davis. This does not appear to bode well for immediate career growth. Since I am early in my career and career growth is important to me, I have elected to seek opportunities elsewhere.

Should one of your clients be looking for a young, ambitious Procurement professional who has a strong work ethic and a demonstrated drive for bringing continuous improvement to business systems and processes, I hope that you will contact me.

Thank you for reviewing my credentials, and I hope to hear from you in the near future.

Very truly yours,

Michael T. English
Michael T. English

Enclosure

SCOTT M. BEATTY
818 Kimberly Lane
Chadds Ford, PA 19382

March 25, 1996

Technical Placement, Inc.
125 North C Street
Chicago, IL 17283

Dear Sir/Madam:

I am an honors engineering student at Bucknell University and will be graduating with a B.S. in Mechanical Engineering in May of this year.

I am in search of an entry-level position as a Project Engineer in the central engineering department of a manufacturing company. I would enjoy being involved with the engineering, installation and start-up of manufacturing equipment as well as general plant facilities engineering work.

Besides my academic achievement, I have been active in athletics and have been a member of the Varsity Crew Team for the last three years. I have a balanced perspective and maintain involvement in a wide range of diverse activities.

Last summer I was an Engineering Intern with the E.I. DuPont Company, where I worked in their central engineering department as a Design Engineer in support of plant capital projects. Although I enjoyed working at DuPont, unfortunately there is a hiring freeze that will not allow the opportunity for employment at this time.

Should one of your client companies have room in their organization for a bright, eager, young Project Engineer, I would appreciate a call. Thank you for your time and consideration.

Sincerely

Scott M. Beatty

Scott M. Beatty

Enclosure

J. Thomas Wainwright
132 Wildflower Lane
Wilton, CT 16283

September 26, 1997

Ms. Wilma G. Larson
The Landshire Group, Inc.
100 East Bay Circle
New Haven, CT 18273

Dear Ms. Larson:

My company has recently been sold, and the new owners have chosen to manage the business themselves. I am therefore looking for a new opportunity in a senior operating role such as President & C.E.O, C.O.O, or Vice President & General Manager.

While I would prefer to remain in the medical surgical products or consumer health & beauty aids industries, where I have been particularly successful, I would also be interested in pursuing other areas with a company interested in my experience and abilities. Additionally, I would be open to new start-up business opportunities offering a "sweat equity" position as a General Manager.

If you currently have a search assignment that fits these requirements, and you feel my background is appropriate, I would be pleased to hear from you.

My compensation requirements are in the low six figure range, and I am open to relocation for a suitable opportunity.

Thank you for your consideration.

Sincerely,

J. Thomas Wainwright

J. Thomas Wainwright

JTW/mar

Enclosure

JANE E. FAIRHAVEN
12-D Village Park Apts.
215 Old Mill Road
Portland, ME 16284

August 21, 1994

Mr. Lyndon R. Robbins
Scientific Placement, Inc.
123 Boat House Row
Boston, MA 17294

Dear Mr. Robbins:

Flagstaff Paper Company has recently announced a 25% cutback in its Technology Department. Unfortunately, as one of the least senior employees, I will be affected.

I hold a B.S. degree in Electrical Engineering from the University of Maine and have 2 years experience as a Development Engineer in Flagstaff's Control Systems Development Group. In this capacity I work with the Process Development Group in the first-time application of computer control systems to novel, state-of-the-art paper making and converting processes.

The following are some of my accomplishments:

- Engineered entire process control system for prototype
  nonwoven materials manufacturing process.

- Assisted Central Engineering with the first time scale-up
  of new diaper converting process, with responsibility for
  leading scale-up of distributed control systems.

- Engineered motor control system for new pilot scale paper
  machine.

I have a strong background in the design, engineering, installation and start-up of a wide range of instrumentation and control systems. I have the ability to apply this knowledge to both pilot and full-scale manufacturing equipment. I am equally at home with both chemical and mechanical process applications.

My resume is enclosed for your review. I am seeking a Control Systems Engineering position in either a plant manufacturing or research laboratory setting, and would welcome the opportunity to talk with any of your client companies for whom my background and interests are an appropriate fit.

Compensation requirements are in the $55,000 to $60,000 range, and I am open to opportunities with any of your clients located in the New England States.

Thank you for your consideration, and I hope to hear from you in the near future.

Sincerely,

Jane E. Fairhaven

Jane E. Fairhaven

JEF/sam

Enclosure

ALLAN D. MARKS

102 Puritan Lane, Pilgrim Place, PA 19827

April 19, 1995

Ms. Dorothy Wentworth
The Wentworth Agency
100 Congress Walk
Washington, DC 18273

Dear Ms. Wentworth:

Enclosed please find my resume, which details a short but highly successful career in sales and marketing.

Currently, I am a Sales Representative in eastern Pennsylvania for Bachman Metals, a $100 million manufacturer of metal fasteners sold to the hardware trade in the Northeastern U.S.

During my first 2 years selling for Bachman I have more than doubled the sales volume for my territory, going from an annual volume of $10 million to over $22 million. The company is obviously very pleased with my performance!

Unfortunately, Bachman is a family-owned company and long-range development opportunities appear rather limited. As I look at the senior level positions within the company (Director level and above), it has become painfully clear that being a member of the Bachman family is an absolute prerequisite. It is clear, therefore, that I must move on with my career.

Please review the enclosed resume against your current search assignments for sales and marketing personnel. I have an excellent track record and will be a strong producer for any of your clients who can use my background and experience.

Compensation requirements are in the $50,000 range, and I am receptive to relocation in the Northeastern U.S.

Thank you for your consideration.

Sincerely,

Allan D. Marks

Allan D. Marks

ADM/rea

Enclosure

JAMES P. DAVENPORT
2 Roseview Lane
New Garden, NJ 18337

March 29, 1994

Mr. Leland L. Bane
Bane & Greer, Inc.
150 Northwood Circle
Trenton, NJ 18339

Dear Mr. Bane:

With today's economic environment and continued pressure on debt, cash flow, and profitability, companies need people who can make a difference.

I can help. My credentials are strong in Finance, Treasury, and Business Development/Planning. My track record demonstrates exceptional financial, business, and leadership skills. For example:

- After being asked to corral a renegade marketing group, I added numerous controls and won the confidence of marketing by being a business partner. The results - increases of over 25% in sales and 50% in profits. Today, we are taking ownership of additional product lines with a target of $290 million.

- After the merger, I was asked to redesign the cash management network and U.S. order review process. The results - $37 million annual savings, tighter controls, and greater customer satisfaction.

- By working closely with investment bankers, developed innovative financing and investment programs saving $1.3 million per year.

Now I seek a new, more challenging career option. I can produce similar results elsewhere. Perhaps for one of your valued clients.

If I am a fit for one of your current search assignments, I welcome the opportunity to meet with you. Thank you for your consideration.

Sincerely,

James P. Davenport

James P. Davenport

Enclosure

ALICE K. BASSETT

816 General Howe Drive, Chadds Ford, PA 19382

October 15, 1997

Mr. Sangho Back
Senior Partner
Back, Brubaker & Associates
1345 Market Street
Philadelphia, PA 19317

Dear Mr. Back:

Enclosed is my updated resume, which outlines my 15+ years experience in MIS.

The focus of my career has been on the development, implementation, and integration of management information systems in four major industries: Health Care, Government, Retail and Manufacturing.

I can provide numerous references from both my current employer, as well as current and past clients, regarding my achievements and contributions.

Please contact me at my office (215) 875-2837 or home (215) 696-5529 with any questions you may have concerning my qualifications.

Thank you for your consideration, and I look forward to hearing from you regarding appropriate opportunities that may exist with your clients.

Sincerely,

Alice K. Bassett

Alice K. Bassett

Enclosure

JOYCE M. MASON

300 Wellington Circle
Caldwell, NJ 18273

Home: (908) 873-1928
Office: (212) 229-0985

May 22, 1994

Mr. Bradley F. Witherspoon
The Continental Group, Inc.
500 East 45th Street
New York, NY 18274

Dear Mr. Witherspoon:

During the past eight years I have played a major role in revitalizing the chemicals and specialties businesses of the Wothington Corporation, in New York City.

Following an initial assignment as Director of Sales for the Chemicals Division, I was promoted to division General Manager, taking P&L responsibility for several key businesses including management of 3 foreign subsidiaries.

My team's efforts contributed to the major growth in sales, profit contribution, and return on investment of the division, recently renamed the Specialty Products Division.

As the result of the recent sale of this division, I have elected to make a career change and am writing to ask your help. A resume which details my accomplishments at Wothington Corporation, as well as my eight years at Dow Chemical, is attached.

Compensation and location are secondary to opportunity. Ideally, I'd like an assignment at either the general management or senior corporate marketing/sales management level, with an opportunity to match or better my 1993 total cash compensation of $136,000.

If my background should match any of your current or near future search assignments, I'll be pleased to meet with you at your convenience. Thank you for your consideration.

Sincerely,

Joyce M. Mason

Joyce M. Mason

Enclosure

KENNETH B. BARTON
135 East Willow Lane
Torrington, CT 14396
(203) 997-2846

July 16, 1995

Ms. Barbara R. Wilson
Senior Partner
Wilson & Wade, Inc.
301 Fairview Blvd.
New Haven, CT 14839

Dear Ms. Wilson:

If one of your client companies is in search of a seasoned, results-oriented senior sales executive to lead their sales and marketing function, you may want to give careful consideration to my qualifications for the position.

Review of the enclosed resume will reveal that I have over fifteen years of sales management experience, with demonstrated leadership ability in directing and motivating sales organizations to consistently achieve record sales performance.
In my last three positions, for example, the functions that I have managed have set new sales records each and every year, with an average increase of nearly 20% per year!

My qualifications include an M.B.A. in Marketing from the University of Connecticut and nearly eighteen years in consumer product sales. For the last four years I have been Regional Sales Manager for Lever Brothers in the Northeast Region, where I have managed a 80 person sales organization that covers a 10 state area.

My current compensation is $125,000, consisting of a base salary of $95,000 and bonus of $30,000. I am seeking a position at the national sales or sales/marketing level with broader accountability and the opportunity for substantial earnings improvement.

I would be pleased to meet with you to further discuss my credentials and to explore appropriate management opportunities with your clients. Thank you for your consideration, and I look forward to hearing from you.

Sincerely,

Kenneth B. Barton

Kenneth B. Barton

KBB/daf

Enclosure

JANET T. MONOHAN

62 White Cloud Lane
Waverly, NH 86724

Home: (426) 857-1284
Office:(426) 977-2424

August 22, 1996

Mr. Glen K. Thorston
President
The Thorston Group, Inc.
22 Harbour View Towers
604 Plymouth Street
Boston, MA 18374

Dear Mr. Thorston:

My research indicates that your firm specializes in executive search consulting in the financial field. Since I am in search of a position in financial management, I have therefore enclosed my resume for your review against the current needs of your clients.

Briefly, my credentials include an M.B.A. in Finance from the University of Vermont and ten years experience in finance with Barrington Industries, where I am now Manager of Corporate Finance. Barrington Industries, as you may know, is a $500 million manufacturer of floor coverings. In this capacity, I manage a 6 person department with functional responsibility for domestic & international finance, money & banking, financial planning & analysis and treasury.

It appears that my career has peaked here at Barrington, since the current Chief Financial Officer is only two years my senior and is planning to remain with the company. I am therefore seeking a position as Chief Financial Officer with a small to medium-sized manufacturing company, where I can report to the Chief Executive Officer and assume total responsibility for the firm's financial function.

My compensation requirement are in the $100,000 to $115,000 range.

Thank you for reviewing my credentials. I will look forward to hearing from you should you feel I would be a suitable candidate for one of your current or future search assignments.

Very truly yours,

Janet T. Monohan

Janet T. Monohan

Enclosure

DAVID C. PARKER
125 Deep Creek Road
Asheville, NC 17224
(415) 855-9124

July 15, 1996

Mr. Frank B. Breslin
Warner, Breslin & Roe, Inc.
200 Parkway Blvd., NE
Marietta, GA 12682

Dear Mr. Breslin:

I am advised by one of my colleagues that your firm has some specialization in conducting executive search assignments in the field of distribution management. I am pleased, therefore, to forward a copy of my resume for review against your current search assignments in this field.

My qualifications include a B.A. in Business Administration from the University of North Carolina and 18 years experience in distribution management, most of which has been with Burlington Industries, where I am currently corporate Manager of Warehousing & Distribution. In this capacity, I report to the Vice President of Logistics and manage a 350 employee, 12 warehouse transportation and distribution function for this $6 billion corporation.

Under my leadership Burlington has realized over $25 million in annual cost savings during the last 3 years alone, as I have streamlined distribution operations and implemented far-reaching strategies aimed at productivity improvement. I am currently directing 4 major new initiatives that should add another $8 to $10 million annual cost savings to the bottom line over the next 2 years.

Perhaps one of your clients might be interested in my ability to bring similar cost savings and efficiencies to their operations. If so, I would welcome the opportunity to meet with you to explore this possibility.

I am seeking a position at the Director level in distribution management with full accountability for a company's distribution planning and operations. Compensation requirements are in the $85,000 to $100,000 range, dependent upon location and nature of the position.

Thank you for your consideration, and I look forward to hearing from you should you have an appropriate opportunity to discuss with me.

Sincerely,

David C. Parker

David C. Parker

Enclosure

JOEL C. KLEINBAUM
136 Wickersham Road
Midland, MI 13283
(319) 774-2231

September 2, 1995

Ms. Sandra T. Willingham
Willingham, Cosby & Smith
135 Lake Shore Drive
Chicago, IL 15224

Dear Ms. Willingham:

I understand that your company enjoys an excellent reputation as a retained executive search firm in the marketing field. Perhaps you may have an active search assignment for a senior marketing executive with my credentials.

My qualifications include an M.B.A. in Marketing from the University of Michigan and some 16 years marketing and sales experience in the specialty chemicals field. Currently Director of Marketing for the Specialty Chemicals Division of Dow Chemical Company, I manage a staff of 12 brand managers, market analysts and research support personnel in the marketing of a wide range of specialty chemicals sold to numerous industrial applications.

Over my last 3 years in this position, we have successfully introduced over 15 products accounting for over $400 million in new sales. All but one product entry has either reached or exceeded sales expectations, with better than half the products exceeding first year goals by more than 25%.

I am now seeking a position as either vice president or director of marketing and sales at the corporate level. Obviously my strength is in the chemical or specialty chemicals field. Compensation requirements are in the $140+ range, and I will consider relocation to most areas of the country.

Should you have an appropriate search assignment that is a match for my qualifications and interests, I would welcome a call. Thank you for your consideration.

Sincerely,

Joel C. Kleinbaum

Joel C. Kleinbaum

Enclosure

ALLISON D. KLUGER

102 Whalebone Road, Portland, ME 18239

January 16, 1995

Mr. Walter T. Johnson
Johnson Associates
205 Wellsby Road
Portland, ME 18239

Dear Mr. Johnson:

As an employment agency specializing in the recruitment of engineering talent for the pulp and paper industry, you may have some interest in my background. A resume is enclosed for your reference.

Briefly, I am a mechanical engineer with strong project background in the converting of coated and fine papers. I hold a B.S. degree from the University of Maine - Orono, and have spent the last 5 years as a project engineer with the Carver Paper Company at the Westbrook Mill. As you are likely aware, this mill is currently for sale and future career opportunities are therefore uncertain.

I am seeking a position as a senior project engineer or engineering manager within the paper industry, with particular interest in either papermaking or converting. Assignments in general mill engineering would not be of interest.

I am completely open to relocation, and my salary requirements are in the $65,000 to $70,000 range.

Since my employer is unaware of my decision to make a change, I would like to ask that my candidacy be handled with appropriate discretion.

Thank you for your assistance, and I look forward to hearing from you should you locate a suitable opportunity which you feel may be of interest to me.

Very truly yours,

Allison D. Kluger

Enclosure

DAVID W. PIERSON
306 Sheldon Way
Marietta, GA 12847

March 21, 1997

Mr. Kevin F. Martin
President
Martin, Reardon & Gier, Inc.
235 Selby Road, NE
Atlanta, GA 13857

Dear Mr. Martin:

I have recently learned of your firm's specialization in executive search consulting in the field of operations management. Enclosed, therefore, please find a copy of my resume for review against current or future searches that you may be conducting on behalf of a client organization.

My qualifications include a B.S. in Mechanical Engineering from Georgia Tech, followed by an M.B.A. from M.I.T.'s Sloan School of Business. Since graduation from Sloan in 1990, I have been with the General Electric Company in manufacturing management in the company's Small Motors Division.

In the last 7 years since joining G.E., I have experience rapid advancement starting with a position as a Manufacturing Supervisor at a small motors manufacturing facility in Rochester, New York and culminating with my current assignment as General Manager for a 1,200 employee manufacturing facility located in Atlanta, Georgia.

Details of my various assignments and specific accomplishments are highlighted on the enclosed resume.

I am seeking a senior level manufacturing position at the director or vice president level, with full P&L responsibility for a multi-plant operation. My preference would be to remain within the electrical field, since I already have 7 years invested in this industry. Compensation requirements are in the $125,000 base range plus bonus.

Should one of your clients be looking for a fast-track manufacturing executive with excellent experience and solid accomplishments in the electrical field, I would appreciate hearing from you.

Thank you for your consideration.

Sincerely,

David W. Pierson

David W. Pierson

Enclosure

4

Advertising Response Cover Letters

Employment advertising has long been a major source of jobs for those engaged in a job-hunting campaign. Although specific estimates may vary, it is believed that print advertising, whether in the newspaper or a professional/trade journal, accounts for in the neighborhood of 10 to 14 percent of all jobs that are found.

Knowing how to effectively respond to recruitment advertising is, therefore, an important element of one's job hunting effort. How effectively one responds to such advertising has a definite bearing on whether or not an employment interview will follow. Poorly written letters that contain improper grammar and/or lack adequate focus can, in most cases, be counted on to ruin employment chances. By contrast, well-written cover letters can often make the difference and be a key factor in helping to land that all important employment interview.

THE ADVANTAGE

The key advantage of the advertising cover letter, when compared to the general broadcast letter used when making a mass mailing to either companies or search firms, is that the letter's author knows exactly what the employer is seeking. Sadly, this is a key point that falls on deaf ears in far too many cases.

I have been completely amazed how many job seekers choose to ignore the specifics of employer's requirements, as stated in the ad, and go on endlessly to describe qualifications and experience factors that are of little or no interest whatsoever to would-be employers. What a shame to be blind to such a golden opportunity!

Unfortunately, such behavior is reminiscent of the salesperson who doesn't take the time to "qualify" the buyer. By this, I mean that the sales representative fails to query the buyer sufficiently at the beginning of the sales presentation to understand what factors are "key motivators" that will cause the buyer to actually buy the product. The result is that the salesperson drones on and on about the product's many features, but fails to cover those features important to the buying decision. The result is "no sale".

By contrast, the successful sales representative first determines what product attributes are most important to the buyer's purchasing decision. By focusing the sales presentation on these "motivating factors", the representative substantially increases probability of a sale.

BEN FRANKLIN BALANCE SHEET

A good technique to use when preparing to write an advertising response cover letter is the Ben Franklin Balance Sheet. This approach is essentially used to "qualify" the buyer (the employer) and to force yourself to focus only on those candidate qualifications that are important to the employer's hiring decision.

To use this approach, simply draw a line down the center of a piece of tablet-sized paper. Label the left column "employer's requirements". Title the right column "my qualifications".

Now carefully review the employment advertisement line-by-line, and list each of the employer's specific requirements on the left side of your balance sheet. Order and prioritize these on the basis of the emphasis that the employer appears to place on each of these key qualification factors in the actual ad. Key words such as "must have", "prefer", "highly desirable", and so on often provide strong clues about the importance the employer attaches to certain candidate qualifications. Also, the order in which these qualifications are presented in the advertisement is frequently suggestive of their relative importance, with the employer listing "most critical" qualifications first and "least important" requirements last.

Now, using your resume as the basis, prepare a list of those qualifications that you possess that coincide with the employer's requirements. These should be systematically recorded on the right side of your balance sheet under the heading "my qualifications" and adjacent to the relevant employer's requirements.

This simple analysis now places you in an excellent position to write a very effective cover letter. The basic data is readily available and is listed in the order of its importance to the employer. You are now ready to "make the sale".

LETTER COMPONENTS

Review of the sample cover letters which comprise the bulk of this chapter will reveal that the advertising response cover letter contains certain key elements. These are:

1. Reference to advertisement
2. Expression of interest in position

3. Comparison of employer's requirements with personal qualifications
4. Salary requirements statement (optional)
5. Request for response or interview
6. Statement of appreciation

Review of the many sample letters in this chapter will illustrate different ways these elements can be effectively incorporated into the advertising response cover letter.

TWO FORMATS

The advertising response cover letter normally utilizes one of two formats: The *linear* format or the *literary* format. Review of the sample resumes provided in this chapter will reveal several approaches to the use of each.

The *linear* approach is generally used when the author wants to highlight that he or she has all of the key qualifications required by the employer. In such cases the writer provides a line-by-line (linear) listing of these qualifications. Such a linear approach tends to highlight these qualifications and facilitates the employer's direct comparison with its own requirements. This type format plays directly off the stated candidate requirements contained in the employment ad and, if well presented, should systematically lead the employer to the obvious conclusion—that you are well-qualified for the position and are worthy of an employment interview.

The literary format, on the other hand, is most frequently used when the author does not possess all of the key qualifications stated in the advertisement. In such cases the linear approach is studiously avoided, and the writer should use the literary (or paragraph) approach.

Here again, as with the linear format, the letter's author will wish to draw a parallel between his or own qualifications and those which the employer is seeking. By making this comparison using the literary approach, however, it is far less obvious to the employer that certain of these key qualifications are missing. By contrast, use of the linear approach would serve to highlight this void and make it easier for the employer to routinely "screen you out."

The Ben Franklin Balance Sheet will serve you well when choosing which of these two formats to use. Review of this balance sheet will make it clear which of the employer's qualifications you are missing and should make it fairly obvious which of these two letter formats will therefore best serve your needs.

The balance of this chapter contains several examples of employment advertisements, along with sample cover letter responses. You will note how these letters effectively employ the comparison techniques discussed in this chapter. Careful study of these sample letters should enable you to construct highly effective cover letters that significantly enhance the probabilities of landing employment interviews.

ELISE MARKS
100 Bay View Drive
Berkeley, CA 16284

June 24, 1996

Y-34
P.O. Box 2940
Philadelphia, PA 19104

Dear Sir/Madam:

Your ad for a Manufacturing Cost Accountant in the June 12th issue of *The Philadelphia Inquirer* interests me. I am therefore forwarding my resume for your review.

As my resume will demonstrate, I would appear to have excellent qualifications for your opening. Please consider the following:

- B.A. Accounting, Michigan State, 1993

- C.P.A., May, 1994

- 1 Year, Auditor, Coopers & Lybrant

- 1 Year, Cost Accountant, Scott Paper Company
    (Chester, PA Plant)

- Well Versed in Standard Cost Accounting Practices

My salary requirements are in the high $30K range.

Should you agree that my background is a good match for your requirements, I would welcome the opportunity to meet with you personally. I can be reached on a confidential basis during the day at (718) 996-5128.

Thank you for your consideration, and I look forward to hearing from you.

Sincerely,

Elise Marks

Elise Marks

Enclosure

CORPORATE
CONTROLLER

PET Chow, Inc. is a $250 million manufacturer of dog food product with distribution throughout the Northeastern United States. We are a 20 year old company whose sales and profits have nearly tripled in the last 3 years alone.

The position of Corporate Controller reports to the Chief Financial Officer with responsibility for preparation of all quarterly and annual consolidated returns, S.E.C. reporting, accounts receivable, accounts payable, cost accounting, tax research & preparation, credit and audit. Reporting to this position are 4 managers and a staff of 12 professional and support personnel.

This position requires a B.S. in Accounting and at least five years corporate accounting management experience in a multi-plant, multi-state manufacturing environment. Must be thoroughly versed in preparation of consolidated statements, S.E.C. requirements and standard accounting practices. A CPA and at least 2 years public accounting experience also required.

Highly competitive salary and attractive executive bonus program are provided.Comprehensive benefits program also furnished.

For consideration, please forward resume to:

PET Chow, Inc.
P.O. Box 130
Atlanta, GA 18273

Attention: David Wexler

Equal Opportunity Employer, M/F

126 Van Buren Street
Dayton, OH 28397

April 30, 1994

Mr. David Wexler
PET Chow, Inc.
P.O. Box 130
Atlanta, GA 18273

Dear Mr. Wexler:

I am submitting my resume in response to your April 28th ad in the *Atlanta Journal* for a Corporate Controller. This sounds like an interesting position, and I would welcome the opportunity to discuss it with you personally.

It would appear that my qualifications are an excellent match for your requirements.

In keeping with your specification, I hold a B.S. in Accounting from Boston College and have over five years corporate accounting experience with the Bently Corporation, a manufacturer of canned vegetables. Bently has 8 manufacturing facilities located in 6 states.

As Manager of Corporate Accounting, I am responsible for preparation of the company's consolidated returns on both a quarterly and annual basis. I am well-trained in standard accounting procedures and thoroughly versed in S.E.C. requirements.

I completed my C.P.A. in 1984, while an Auditor with Price Waterhouse. My credentials include over three years public accounting experience.

I believe that I am exceptionally well-qualified for the position advertised, and that I could make a meaningful contribution to your company. I hope that we will have the opportunity to meet to further discuss the specifics of your requirements.

Thank you for your consideration.

Sincerely,

Laura Woodcock

Laura Woodcock

LW/rb

Enclosure

LEONARD B. WILLIAMSON

143 North Camp Road
Wilmington, NC 28374

Office: (218) 875-9872
Home: (218) 336-9728

March 31, 1997

Mr. Robert Johnson
Employment Manager
General Chemical Company, Inc.
300 Chemical Way
Flint, MI 18238

Dear Mr. Johnson:

Your ad in the March 28th edition of the *Detroit Press* for Sales Representatives - Specialty Chemicals caught my eye. This sounds like an exciting opportunity that is very much in keeping with my career objectives, and I would appreciate the chance to meet with you to discuss this opportunity further.

Careful review of your requirements suggests that I am well-qualified for this position. Consider the following:

- B.S. Degree in Chemical Engineering

- 3 Years Selling Specialty Chemicals to the Corrugated Industry

- General Knowledge of Papermaking Processes

- Strong Technical Problem-Solving Skills
  (Used as Regional Resource on Tough Customer Problems)

My interpersonal skills are solid, and I am frequently called upon to make important customer presentations due to my excellent communication and presentation skills.

In addition, you might like to know that I was the leading Sales Representative in the Southern Region in 1996.

Hopefully you are convinced that I have the talent and motivation required to make a strong contribution to General Chemical, and we will have the opportunity to meet in the near future.

Thank you for your consideration, and I look forward to hearing from you.

Very truly yours,

Leonard B. Williamson

Leonard B. Williamson

Enclosure

DIRECTOR

SALES & MARKETING

Fin Tube, Inc., a leading manufacturer of copper refrigeration and automotive tubing is seeking a Director of Sales & Marketing to manage its corporate marketing/sales function.

This position reports to the President and is responsible for developing and leading the strategy needed to support the company's aggressive growth plans. Products are sold both direct and through distributor network to O.E.M. accounts.

We seek a degreed executive with a strong background in marketing and sales management to OEM accounts. Must be a talented leader/motivator with a solid track record in continuously achieving sales objectives. Must be good strategic thinker who can contribute to the management of the business as a member of the senior management team.

If qualified and interested in this position, please send resume and salary history to:

Martha F. Farlington
Executive Vice President

Fin Tube, Inc.
200 East Commerce Blvd.
Tampa, FL 18273

Equal Opportunity Employer, M/F

PHILLIP R. ZANFAGNA

235 East Willow Lane
Falls Church, VA 16284

Home: (315) 874-2136
Office: (315) 275-9087

October 16, 1995

Ms. Martha F. Farlington
Executive Vice President
Fin Tube, Inc.
200 East Commerce Blvd.
Tampa, FL 18273

Dear Ms. Farlington:

I am forwarding my resume in response to your October 15th ad in the *Tampa Herald* for a Director - Sales & Marketing. This position sounds quite interesting, and I would appear to fit the candidate specification as detailed in your ad.

Specifically, I hold an MBA in Marketing and have over 10 years marketing and sales management experience selling to O.E.M. accounts. As Director of Marketing for Fuel Jet Carburetors, I manage a 30 employee marketing and field sales organization selling automotive carburetors to car and truck engine manufacturers through both a distributor network and direct.

During the last five years in this capacity, my marketing and sales strategies have led to a 250% increase in sales volume coupled with a profit increase of nearly 300%. I am known for being a key contributor to the business planning process and am credited with revitalizing and motivating the marketing and sales organization through creative leadership.

I would welcome the opportunity to meet with you to explore how I might bring added value to Fin Tube's marketing and sales effort through solid strategic planning and effective managerial leadership.

My current compensation is $125,000 ($100,000 base salary plus $25,000 bonus). I also have a company furnished automobile and other minor executive perks.

Thank you for your consideration. I look forward to hearing from you.

Sincerely,

Phillip R. Zanfagna

Phillip R. Zanfagna

PRZ/csp

Enclosure

FINANCIAL ANALYST

Fortune 200 consumer products company seeks Financial Analyst for Corporate Planning Group.

Position reports to the Manager of Strategic Planning and will participate in the evaluation of various strategic business options including: acqusitions & mergers, new business development, and expansion/consolidation of existing businesses. Will regularly interface with senior executive officers, including the presentation of study findings and recommendations regarding alternate business strategies.

Successful candidate will hold an MBA from a highly quantitative business school with emphasis in Finance. Must have excellent interpersonal and communications skills, including the presence and poise needed to interface effectively with executive level management. Some prior experience in merger and acquisitions analysis helpful.

Please forward resume and salary requirements to:

Ms. Sandra G. Lanstrum
Administrative Employment Manager

JOHNSON & JOHNSON
1 Johnson & Johnson Plaza
New Brunswick, NJ 12938

Equal Opportunity Employer, M/F

JUDITH L. KRUG

20 Winding Lane   Home: (214) 357-9574
Windsor, WI 18274   Office: (214) 225-9086
_____

February 12, 1994

Ms. Sandra G. Lanstrum
Administrative Employment Manager
Johnson & Johnson
1 Johnson & Johnson Plaza
New Brunswick, NJ 12938

Dear Ms. Lanstrum:

I noted your ad for a Financial Analyst in this Sunday's edition of the
Madison Gazette with a great deal of interest. Your candidate description
appears to be an excellent match with my personal profile.

Please consider the following:

- MBA, University of Wisconsin, Honors Graduate
  (Finance Major)

- Excellent Communication Skills:

    Debate Team President, 1993 & 1994
    Actress, 4 Plays
    English 101 (Freshman Composition), Grade = A

- Evidence of Interpersonal/Leadership Skills

    Sorority President, 2 Years
    Sorority Vice President, 1 Year

My extracurricular activities and summer work experience have enabled me to
develop the poise and maturity needed to effectively relate to senior level
management. Additionally, I assisted in merger and acquisitions analysis
during my summer employment with the DuPont Company.

I believe that these qualifications, along with my drive and enthusiasm,
would make me an excellent candidate for your opening. I would hope to have
the opportunity to meet with you during a visit to Johnson & Johnson.

Thank you for your consideration.

Very truly yours,

Judith L. Krug

Judith L. Krug

Enclosure

VICE PRESIDENT
FINANCE

We are a $250 million manufacturer of electronic components for the defense industry. A large federal contract has necessitated that we double our size in the next 18 months, requiring total restructuring of our finances.

This position reports to the Chief Financial Officer with full responsibility for day-to-day direction of the company's financial functions including money & banking, domestic finance, international finance and credit.

We seek a seasoned financial manager with a minimum of 10 years experience in the defense manufacturing industry. Must be thoroughly versed in financial theory and highly innovative in the approaches to raising capital and restructuring corporate debt load.

Excellent interpersonal, communications and managerial skills required.

Send resume and compensation requirements to:

Box 2534
THE NEW YORK TIMES
600 Park Avenue
New York, NY 14928

DAVID R. APPLER
102 Gregg Street
Shillington, PA 19284

July 18, 1997

Box 2534
New York Times
600 Park Avenue
New York, NY 14928

Dear Sir/Madam:

I am interested in talking with you concerning your need for a Vice President of Finance, as described in your July 18th ad in the *New York Times*. This appears to be an exciting opportunity, and I appear to have the profile that you are seeking.

My resume is enclosed for your review and consideration.

As specified in your advertisement, I am a seasoned financial manager with over 10 years experience in the defense manufacturing industry. Specifically, I am Manager of Corporate Finance with Jetstar Electronics, a supplier of weaponry guidance systems for military vehicles.

My credentials include an MBA in Finance from the University of Chicago, and I am well-schooled in financial theory and its applications.

As evidence of my innovation, despite loss of its AA financial rating and an after tax loss of $20 million in 1995, I was able to secure a $130 million line of credit at prime rate for Jetstar.

By restructuring the corporate debt load and providing the funding for a $100 million capital expansion program, Jetstar was able to "turn the corner" and return to profitability.

Our 1996 after tax profit was $22 million, a healthy 16% ROI! Additionally, our AA financial rating has been restored and Jetstar is now on the "recommended buy" list of several of the nation's leading brokerage houses.

Perhaps I could make a similar contribution to your company. I would welcome the opportunity to explore this possibility during a personal interview.

I appreciate your consideration, and look forward to hearing from you. Thank you.

Sincerely,

David R. Appler

David R. Appler

Enclosure

MARKETING BRAND MANAGER

CONSUMER PRODUCTS

Fortune 200 consumer products company with annual sales of $6.2 billion seeks Marketing Brand Manager for leading hair care product line. Need bright, innovative individual who can revitalize sagging sales and restore product to its dominant market position.

Position requires an MBA in Marketing and 5+ years marketing experience in consumer products industry. Must have demonstrated brand management skills and proven record of significant marketing contribution as measured by sales volume and market share.

Successful candidate will be highly creative, resourceful and possess excellent interpersonal and communications skills. Business team leadership and an appreciation for the participative style of management should be well-evidenced.

Excellent base salary plus participation in management incentive plan are offered, plus a highly competitive benefits package.

For consideration, send resume in to:

Manager of Professional Employment

PERSONAL CARE LABORATORIES, INC.
130 Commerce Drive
Dayton Corporate Center
Dayton, OH 16283

Equal Opportunity Employer, M/F

DEBORAH C. BASS

135 Winham Court, Atlanta, GA 17284

June 26, 1994

Manager of Professional Employment
Personal Care Laboratories, Inc.
130 Commerce Drive
Dayton Corporate Center
Dayton, OH 16283

Dear Sir/Madam:

You sparked my interest with your ad for a Marketing Brand Manager - Consumer Products in today's *Atlanta Journal*. This sounds like an exciting opportunity, and I would appear to have the qualifications you are seeking.

Please consider my credentials as follows:

- MBA in Marketing, Georgia Tech, 1989

- 5 Years Consumer Marketing Experience
  (P&G Corporate Marketing Department)

- Brand Management Marketing Results Include:

    20 point market share increase - Radiant Shampoo
    50% sales increase -- Wash 'N Dry
    14 point market share increase - Today's Woman

I am noted for being an effective communicator and an excellent team player. I frequently serve as facilitator during business team meetings, and am skilled at maximizing group participation and creating a feeling of "team ownership" of marketing plans and strategies. I am a strong advocate of the "participative" style of management and enjoy excellent interpersonal relationships with others.

Should you have an interest in me, I would be pleased to visit Personal Care Laboratories to further explore this opportunity with you and the members of your Marketing Staff.

Thank you for consideration, and I look forward to hearing from you in the near future.

Sincerely,

Deborah C. Bass

Deborah C. Bass

Enclosure

JOSEPH M. BALLENTYNE
204 Pleasant Point Road
Muskeegon, MI 18275

September 22, 1997

Ms. Linda B. Bankstrom
Vice President Marketing
Micrographics International, Inc.
1525 Wolverine Street
Ann Arbor, MI 18374

Dear Ms. Bankstrom:

Your September 21st ad in the Grand Rapids Inquirer for a Director of Marketing has stimulated considerable interest on my part. I am therefore submitting my resume for your review and consideration.

Much of my background closely parallels your specific requirements, and I would appear to be well-qualified for this opportunity.

I hold an MBA in Marketing and am currently Manager of Marketing for DRC Systems, Inc., a $300 million manufacturer of computer systems sold to banks, insurance companies and governmental agencies. I am familiar with the financial record keeping requirements of these organizations.

Under my marketing leadership, DRC Systems has more than doubled its annual sales in the last 5 years. This growth has been driven by the highly successful introduction of two new product lines -- DRC System 4 and System 5. Additionally, System 1 has been successfully repositioned in the market, resulting in a 15% gain in market share.

My knowledge of your target markets, coupled with demonstrated success in the marketing of major new system products, strongly suggests that I could make a significant contribution to your marketing and business objectives. Perhaps we could meet to more thoroughly explore this possibility.

My compensation requirements are in the low six figure range.

I appreciate your consideration, and look forward to the possibility of meeting with you and the members of your senior management team. Thank you.

Sincerely,

Joseph M. Ballentyne

Joseph M. Ballentyne

Enclosure

PROJECT ENGINEER

Black & Decker, the world's leader in the manufacture and sale of power tools, seeks Project Engineer for its 1,000 employee manufacturing facility in Baltimore. This is an excellent opportunity for fresh graduate looking for first exposure to plant project engineering.

Position reports to Senior Project Engineer, and is responsible for assisting in the engineering, installation and start-up of small tool manufacturing equipment.

Ideal candidate will have a B.S.in Mechanical Engineering and a strong desire for hands-on project work. Above average academic performance and/or demonstrated leadership potential highly desirable.

Excellent compensation and complete benefits program provided.

Interested candidates should send resume to:

Mr. John C. Harggart
Technical Employment Manager

BLACK & DECKER COMPANY
1300 Prince Blvd.
Columbia, MD 18274

Equal Opportunity Employer, M/F

LOUISE M. VALENTINE
205 West Bridge Avenue
College Park, MD 18272

February 18, 1997

Mr. John C. Harggart
Technical Employment Manager
Black & Decker Company
1300 Prince Blvd.
Columbia, MD 18274

Dear Mr. Harggart:

The position of Project Engineer which you advertised in this Sunday's edition of the *Baltimore Sun* sounds just like the kind of job for which I am looking. Additionally, I would seem to be an excellent match for your requirements.

My qualifications include:

- B.S. in Mechanical Engineering, Un. of Maryland

- Grade Point Average = 3.4/4.0

- Demonstrated Leaderhip Includes:

    Captain, Varsity Swim Team, 1997
    Vice President, KD Sorority, 1996
    Vice President, A.S.M.E., 1996

I have always enjoyed hands-on as opposed to theoretical works. This is well demonstrated through several of my hobbies: auto repair, furniture building, construction & remodeling, etc.

Additionally, my co-op assignments as Assistant Plant Project Engineer at Wellbar Corporation have provided me with practical, hands-on plant project engineering   experience.

May I have the opportunity to meet with you and the members of your Plant Engineering Staff?

I look forward to hearing from you.

Sincerely,

Louise M. Valentine

Louise M. Valentine

Enclosure

DIRECTOR OF ENGINEERING

Major manufacturer of coated papers seeks executive to head its 150 employee central engineering group.

Position reports to the Vice President of Technology and is responsible, through engineering staff, for directing all capital project work - including mill construction, expansions and major rebuild projects. Will manage annual capital projects budget of $400 to $600 million.

Seek seasoned engineering executive with 20+ years experience in the paper industry. Must demonstrate ability to effectively direct and manage sizeable engineering department with large scale, multiple project workload. Must be a a strong advocate/practitioner of participative management and believe in the importance of "employee stakeholders" as the key to employee morale and productivity.

Highly competitive base salary plus executive bonus plan. Excellent range of cafeteria-style benefits also available.

For consideration, please forward complete resume and compensation requirements to:

Ms. Beth Ann Foster
Director of Employment

FILBERT PAPER COMPANY, INC
300 Fox River Blvd.
Green Bay, WI 18273

103 South Marlin Lane
Mobile, AL 12738

August 15, 1996

Ms. Beth Ann Foster
Director of Employment
Filbert Paper Company, Inc.
300 Fox River Blvd.
Green Bay, WI 18273

Dear Ms. Foster:

I am forwarding my resume in response to your August 15th ad in the *Chicago Tribune* for the position of Director of Engineering. This appears to be an exciting opportunity, and one for which I am well-qualified.

As called for in your advertisement, I am a seasoned engineering executive with over 20 years experience in the paper industry. In my current position as Manager of Corporate Engineering for Telstar Paper Company, I direct a 40 employee central engineering group accountable for all capital project work (new equipment installation and rebuilds) at 4 paper manufacturing/converting mills. Our annual capital budget is in the $300 to $500 million range.

Some major capital projects which I have directed include:

- Engineering & Construction of Windsor Mill
  (A 40 TPD Corrugated Plant)
  (Capital Budget = $350 Million)

- Complete Rebuild of 2 Fine Paper Machines -
  Mobile, Alabama Plant
  (Capital Expense = $210 Million)

I am both a strong advocate and practitioner of the "participative" approach to management. I endeavor to involve my subordinates in all aspects of department operations, from strategic planning through day-to-day operations. I have personally led and facilitated several productivity task forces, which have included representation from all levels of the engineering organization. I recognize the value of the "employee stakeholder" concept.

I feel I have the qualifications to make a strong contribution to Filbert Paper Company's Central Engineering Group, and hope that you agree. I would welcome the opportunity to meet with you.

My compensation requirements are in the low $100K range.

I look forward to hearing from you shortly. Thank you.

Sincerely,

Roger P. Hampton

Roger P. Hampton

Enclosure

ADMINISTRATIVE RECRUITER

We seek an experienced recruiter to handle all administrative employment for our $200 million, multi-plant baked goods manufacturing company.

Position reports to the Director of Human Resources, and is responsible for the recruitment and hiring of all administrative, marketing and sales professionals.

Successful candidate will have a college degree coupled with 1 to 2 years experience in a corporate employment function. Should be knowledgeable concerning the cost effective use of employment sources, including college recruiting.

If interested, please forward your resume to:

Mr. Howard C. Becker
Director of Human Resources

WALTERS COOKIE COMPANY
200 North River Road
Minneapolis, MN 18274

Equal Opportunity Employer, M/F

EILEEN M. LLOYD

204 Puritan Road   Home: (215) 437-9037
Plymouth Meeting, PA 19284   Office:(215) 693-4058

                                                    January 12, 1995

Mr. Howard C. Becker
Director of Human Resources
Walters Cookie Company
200 North River Road
Minneapolis, MN 18274

Dear Mr. Becker:

I noted your ad for an Administrative Recruiter in the Sunday edition of
the *Minneapolis Star Ledger* with a great deal of interest. I am planning a
move to the Minneapolis area and would seem to be exceptionally well-
qualified for the position you advertised.

I hold a B.A. degree in English from Bucknell University and have spent the
last 3 years as Employment Manager for Campbell Soup Company, where I have
been heavily involved in the successful recruitment of all administrative
personnel.

My current assignment requires that I deal effectively with a wide range of
recruitment sources. These have included: college recruiting, employment
advertising, employee referral systems, resume data bases, alumni
associations, professional & trade associations, etc.

In the 3 years that I have been in this position, I have reduced agency
fees by 80% (annual savings of $330,000) and reduced the interview-to-hire
ration from 8:1 to 2.5:1. This improved ratio has saved considerable
managerial time and returned an estimated $85,000 per year in candidate
travel expense.

I am well-motivated to continuously bring improvement to the employment
process and to reduce employment costs.

May I have the opportunity of meeting with you during my forthcoming trip
to Minneapolis? I will be in your area from February 6th through the 20th.

Thank you for your consideration, and I look forward to hearing from you
shortly.

                                            Sincerely,

                                            Eileen M. Lloyd
                                            Eileen M. Lloyd

Enclosure

SENIOR VICE PRESIDENT

HUMAN RESOURCES

Internationally-known 12 plant, 12,000 employee, specialty glass manufacturer seeks top Human Resources officer for corporate staff.

Position reports to the President, and is accountable for management of a 28 employee staff. Functional responsibilities include organization design, staffing, training & development, compensation & benefits, employee & labor relations, diversity and safety & hygiene.

Our client seeks a seasoned Human Resources professional with 15+ years experience, including management of a sizeable H.R. staff operation. Requires a Masters degree in Human Resources or Psychology with strengths in organization design & development and labor relations.

Must be a strategic leader capable of orchestrating and leading major cultural change efforts aimed at substantially improving the use and productivity of human assets. Must also be a strong advocate of the participative management philosophy and be capable of providing strategic leadership in the corporate-wide transition from "top down" management to "employee empowered" processes.

Interested candidates, please forward resumes and salary requirements to:

Ms. Denise T. Ragsdale

Steward & Lombard Associates
Executive Search Consultants
1435 East Wilshire Road
Chicago, IL 17284

JOAN E. ZANFAGNA

825 Sunny Lane   Home: (313) 274-1947
Arlington, IL 17374   Office: (313) 726-1818

April 16, 1996

Ms. Denise T. Ragsdale
Steward & Lombard Associates
Executive Search Consultants
1435 East Wilshire Road
Chicago, IL 17284

Dear Ms. Ragsdale:

I was intrigued by your ad in this Sunday's edition of the *Chicago Tribune* and am enclosing my resume for your consideration. It seems that I have some excellent qualifications for this position and that my background should be of strong interest to your client.

I am a heavily seasoned Human Resources professional with an M.S. degree in Psychology and over 15 years experience. In my current position as Director of Human Resources for Wellington Corporation, I manage a staff of 35 and provide a full range of Human Resource services to the corporate staff and 8 manufacturing plants.

In my earlier assignment as Director of Organization Development, I was heavily involved in organization design and development activities. This included a major redesign and restructuring of the corporate staff. I was also instrumental, as a Senior O.D. Consultant, in successfully leading and facilitating a major shift in organization culture from a traditional management system to one that is based on socio-technical concepts.

I have always made a point to stay current with new, evolving Human Resource concepts, and am quick to seize the opportunity to introduce those having positive effect on productivity. I value being a strong strategic contributor and am known for my innovativeness.

My salary requirements are in the low $100K range.

May I have the opportunity of meeting with you to discuss your client's requirements in greater detail? I believe this would prove a mutually beneficial meeting.

I appreciate your consideration, and look forward to hearing from you.

Sincerely,

Joan E. Zanfagna

Joan E. Zanfagna

Enclosure

PRODUCT DEVELOPMENT
ENGINEER

Leading manufacturer of nonwoven materials seeks Product Development Engineer for R&D Group.

Position reports to the Product Development Group Leader in the development of new, air-layed materials to be used as inner and outer barriers for disposable diapers liners and similar proprietary applications.

Requirements include an advanced degree in Chemical Engineering, Materials Science or Polymer Chemistry with 2 to 3 years research experience in nonwovens product development. Strong knowledge of polymer chemistry and fiber structures a must. Exposure to superabsorbant materials technology a definite plus.

Please forward resume along with salary rquirements to:

Dr. Joseph P. Waxler
Director of Administrative Services
Technology Group

Scott Paper Company
Scott Plaza III
Philadelphia, PA 19117

Equal Opportunity Employer, M/F

CARLTON T. JONES

800 Hill Top Road   Home: (284) 775-0943
Kennett Square, PA 19284   Office:(284) 662-1118

August 12, 1994

Dr. Joseph P. Waxler
Director of Administrative Services
Technology Group
Scott Paper Company
Scott Plaza III
Philadelphia, PA 19117

Dear Dr. Waxler:

I was delighted to see your recent advertisement for a Product Development Engineer in the July issue of *Paper World*. It seems that my qualifications and interests are a close match for your requirements. I am equally delighted that the position is local and would not require my relocation.

Interestingly, I am currently working as a Research Scientist for the Paper Chemicals Division of Hercules, Inc., a major supplier of polymers to the nonwovens industry. My principal accountability is the development of novel, new polymer materials for various nonwovens applications, including superabsorbancy. I am thoroughly versed in polymer science and have expert knowledge of fibrous structures (especially nonwoven structures).

I hold a Ph.D. in Chemical Engineering from the University of Michigan and have been awarded 16 U.S. patents having to do with polymeric materials and fibrous structures. Ten of these are in the nonwovens field.

I trust that my qualifications will be of interest to you, and that we may have the opportunity to meet for the purpose of discussing your requirements in greater detail.

My salary requirements are in the mid $70K range, however, I am flexible dependent upon the specifics of the opportunity.

Thank you for your consideration, and I hope to hear from you shortly.

Very truly yours,

Carlton T. Jones

Carlton T. Jones

Enclosure

DIRECTOR PROCESS DEVELOPMENT

We are a Fortune 200, sanitary tissue, personal care and cleaning products company with sales in the $5 billion range. The world leader in the manufacture of towels and tissues, our company has maintained its competitive edge through its commitment to continuous research and development.

We are in need of a Director of Process Development to lead our research efforts in the area of wet-lay sheet formation process development. This position reports to the Vice President of Technology and is responsible for leading a 15 person department in the development of new paper making processes, from bench scale through pilot plant studies.

Position requires a Ph.D in Chemical Engineering, Chemistry, or other relevant technical discipline, and a minimum of 10 years research in paper making process development. Must be thoroughly knowledgeable in the application of twin-wire sheet forming technology and have led successful development programs in the development of novel paper making processes.

Excellent interpersonal, communications and leadership skills are also a requirement.

Please forward complete resume, along with compensation requirements, to:

Mr. David R. Tucker
Employment Manager - Technology

SNYDER PAPER COMPANY
133 Old Mill Road
Wilton, NH 17283

Equal Opportunity Employer, M/F

DONALD C. SMATHERS, Ph.D.

108 Ridge Road, Wilbraham, MA 17264

November 23, 1996

Mr. David R. Tucker
Employment Manager - Technology
Snyder Paper Company
133 Old Mill Road
Wilton, NH 17283

Dear Mr. Tucker:

You ad for a Director of Process Development in the November issue of the *TAPPI Journal* seems a surprisingly good match for my background. I have a strong interest in this position and am therefore submitting my resume for your consideration.

The following listing of my qualifications highlights the closeness of this match:

- Ph.D. in Chemical Engineering

- Twelve (12) Years Paper Making Process Development
  (Tissue and Towel Products)

- Expert in Twin-Wire Sheet Formation (8 Patents)

- Principal Scientist in Development of Revolutionary
  New Transpiration Drying Process

- Research Group Leader for Highly Successful Wet Lay
  Tissue Development Process (5 Patents)

In my current position as Process Development Group Leader, I have been a successful advocate of several new technology concepts, providing solid evidence of both my leadership and communications skills. My ability to relate to others across the organization has frequently been cited as a key strength.

I would appreciate the opportunity to meet with you and the other members of your Technology Staff to explore how my capabilities might be used to further enhance Snyder Paper Company's competitive position in the marketplace.

My compensation requirements are in the low $90K range.

Thank you for reviewing my credentials. I look forward to hearing from you.

Sincerely,

Donald C. Smathers

Donald C. Smathers

Enclosure

MARVIN S. GOODMAN
226 Lakeside Avenue
Utica, NY 17263

August 23, 1994

Ms. Jean R. Maxwell
Director of Human Resources
Precision Metals, Inc.
300 East River Drive
Buffalo, NY 17283

Dear Ms. Maxwell:

I am forwarding my resume in response to your August 23rd ad in the *Buffalo Daily News* for a Systems Analyst. Comparison of my qualifications with your requirements, as specified in this advertisement, suggests that I would be an excellent candidate for this position.

Highlights of my qualifications are:

- B.S. Degree, Computer Science, Syracuse University

- 2 Years Experience, Systems Analyst

- Good Knowledge of General Ledger Accounting Systems
  (Accounting Minor at Syracuse)

- Group Leader for Order Tracking System
  (A $1.5 Million Systems Project)

My qualifications suggest that I should be able to make an immediate and significant contribution to Precision Metals in its evaluation, selection and successful installation of a general ledger accounting system.

Should you agree, I would welcome the opportunity to further explore this opportunity.

Thank you for your consideration, and I look forward to hearing from you.

Very truly yours,

Marvin S. Goodman

Marvin S. Goodman

MSG/bh

Enclosure

122 North Pheasant Run
Columbus, OH 17263

October 15, 1995

Mr. Ronald G. Kratz
Manager of Corporate Employment
National Insurance Company, Inc.
835 Progress Lane
Fort Wayne, IN 12938

Dear Mr. Kratz:

I read your October 14th ad in the *Columbus Dispatch* for a Manager of MIS with a great deal of interest. From your description, this position seems a good match for my skills and capabilities.

I have enclosed my resume for your review and evaluation.

According to this advertisement, you are seeking someone with a degree in Computer Science and a minimum of 12 to 15 years MIS experience with an insurance company, bank or other financial institution. I graduated with a B.S. in Computer Science from Ohio State and have over 15 years MIS experience in the insurance industry.

Further, you state that you are seeking a candidate who has successfully managed a sizeable corporate MIS group and is intimately familiar with all aspects of providing a high level of systems support to a demanding client base in a fast-paced business environment.

As Manger of MIS for Reliance Insurance Company, I direct an 80 employee corporate MIS function providing a full range of systems support to the corporate staff and 135 branch office locations. Our clients are demanding and insist on a high level of support, despite a fast-changing business culture.

Since I am already living in Columbus, this position would not require relocation.

Please review my accomplishments as highlighted on the enclosed resume. Should you agree that I am well-qualified for this position, I would look forward to the opportunity of meeting with you personally to further explore my credentials and your specific requirements.

I can be reached at my office on a confidential basis during the day or at my home in the evening.

Thank you for your consideration.

Sincerely,

Samuel P. Davidson

Samuel P. Davidson

Enclosure

CHEMICALS BUYER

We are a leader in the manufacture and sale of specialty polyurethane foams. Principal customers include the automotive and defense industries.

We seek a Chemicals Buyer to work in the Purchasing Department at our corporate offices in Cleveland, Ohio. This position is responsible for the bulk purchase and delivery of raw material chemicals including resins, TDI, dyes, etc.

Position requires a degreed buyer with 2 or more years experience in chemical purchasing. Must have successfully negotiated large bulk contracts for multi-site manufacturing operations. Should be skilled in the negotiation of long term contracts at extremely favorable terms.

For consideration, please forward you resume and compensation requirements to:

Ms. Margaret Johnson
Director of Materials & Logistics

GENERAL FOAM CORPORATION
200 Airport Road
Fort Wayne, IN 17263

An Equal Opportunity Employer

WILLIAM E. DAVIS
816 Kimberly Lane
West Chester, PA 19382

July 22, 1996

Ms. Margaret Johnson
Director of Materials & Logistics
General Foam Corporation
200 Airport Road
Fort Wayne, IN 17263

Dear Ms. Johnson:

I would appear to be an excellent candidate for the position of Chemicals Buyer, as advertised by General Foam in the July 12th edition of the *Fort Wayne Herald*. Please accept the enclosed resume as an indication of my strong interest in this position.

Comparison of my qualifications with your requirements suggests to me that there is a solid basis for further discussion of this opportunity through a face-to-face interview. Please consider the following highlights from my background:

- B.S. Degree, Chemistry Major, Ohio State

- 4 Years Chemical Purchasing Experience

- Successful Negotiation of Multi-Million Dollar Contracts for 6 Plant Sites

- Excellent Reputation as Skillful Negotiator of Long-Term Contracts at Below Market Rates

My current annual compensation is $58,000, and I would anticipate an increase in the 10% range to warrant a career move at this time.

I would appreciate the opportunity to further discuss this opportunity with you and to mutually explore the contributions I might make to your purchasing function.

Thank you for your consideration, and I look forward to hearing from you.

Very truly yours,

William E. Davis

William E. Davis

Enclosure

VICE PRESIDENT

LOGISTICS MANAGEMENT

Fortune 300 food manufacturer seeks Vice President of Logistics to direct $600 million corporate-wide logistics operation. Functional responsibilities include order entry/tracking, production planning/scheduling, raw materials planning/scheduling, warehousing, distribution and fleet management.

We seek seasoned logistics executive with 20+ years experience in all aspects of logistics and materials management. Must have successfully directed large, complex logistics function for major consumer products or foods company. Must be up-to-date in the application of modern computer systems to materials management.

Position reports to Senior Vice President of Operations and offers a highly competitive compensation and comprehensive benefits program.

Please submit resume and compensation requirements to:

Ms. Martha S. Wilson
Senior Vice President
Human Resources

AMERICAN FOODS CORPORATION
100 Federal Towers
3500 East 45th Street
Chicago, IL 18274

JAMES R. LINK

137 East Meadow Lane   Home: (317) 274-9572
Oakbrook, IL 18372   Office:(317) 977-0941

January 21, 1994

Ms. Martha S. Wilson
Senior Vice President
Human Resources
American Foods Corporation
100 Federal Towers
3500 East 45th Street
Chicago, IL 18274

Dear Ms. Wilson:

As specified in Sunday's ad in the *Chicago Tribune*, you are searching for a
Vice President - Logistics Management. I think that review of the enclosed
resume could well establish that I am the candidate for this position.

Please consider the following highlights of my background :

- Seasoned Logistics Executive With 22 Years Experience

- Director of Logistics, Giant Foods Corporation
  (A $2 billion Food & Beverage Industry Company)

- Manage Staff of 60 Employees in the Day-to-Day
  Operation of the Corporate Logistics Function

- Directed the Selection & Successful Installation of
  a Corporate-Wide Order Entry/Production Scheduling/
  Inventory Management Computer System ($2 Million
  Project)

Over the last five years, I have returned more than $8 million to the
business through the application of innovative cost-savings programs aimed
at improving overall Logistics efficiencies. Perhaps I could make a similar
contribution to American Foods Corporation.

If my background is of interest, I would welcome the opportunity to meet
with you and other appropriate members of your senior management team.

Thank you for considering my credentials, and I look forward to hearing
from you in the near future.

Sincerely,

James R. Link

James R. Link

Enclosure

PUBLIC AFFAIRS ASSOCIATE

Large (1,200 employee) manufacturing site of $8 billion defense manufacturer seeks Public Affairs professional.

This position reports to the Manager of Public Affairs and is responsible for all community affairs activities designed to foster goodwill and positive relationship with the local community. Will assist the Manager in carrying out various legislative affairs activities at both the local and state levels.

Prefer a degree in Public Affairs, Communications, Psychology or other relevant discipline plus 1 or more years in a position requiring considerable public contact. Requires exceptionally strong interpersonal and communications skills as well the image, poise and maturity to effectively deal with corporate executives and high level government officials.

For consideration, please forward resume and salary requirements to:

Human Resources Manager
WELLER ELECTRONICS, INC
300 Park Avenue, SW
Orlando, FL 17294

Equal Opportunity Employer, M/F

WILLIAM HARBSTER

106 Summit Avenue   Home: (215) 872-9483
Sinking Springs, PA 19284   Office: (215) 372-9184

June 25, 1995

Human Resources Manager
Weller Electronics, Inc.
300 Park Avenue, SW
Orlando, FL 17294

Dear Sir/Madam:

Enclosed please find my resume in response to your recent advertisement in the June 24th edition of the *Orlando Sentinel* for a Public Affairs Associate. This position sounds exciting, and I would welcome the opportunity to discuss it further with you.

As my resume will attest, I appear to have excellent qualifications for this position as follow:

- B.A. Degree, Public Affairs, American University

- 2 Years as Administrative Aid to U.S. Senator Richard Schultz

  (Considerable public contact requiring poise, maturity and strong communications skills)

- Seasoned, Skilled Goodwill Ambassador in Building and Maintaining Positive Public Image on Wide Range of Issues.

I feel that I have the knowledge, skills and motivation needed to provide strong support to your Manager of Public Affairs in effectively handling both public affairs and legislative affairs matters. My experience in government should also prove a strong asset to this position.

Should you also agree that my background is a good match for your requirements, I would welcome the opportunity to meet with you to further explore this excellent opportunity. My salary requirements are in the high $40K range.

Please call me on a confidential basis at my office during the day, or a my home in the evening.

I hope that you will view my qualifications favorably and that I will be hearing from you shortly. Thank you.

Sincerely,

William Harbster

William Harbster

Enclosure

COMMUNICATIONS MANAGER

Public Affairs Department of large
commercial bank (52 branch offices)
seeks communications professional to
manage employee publications and
internal employee communications
programs. Will report to the Director
of Public Affairs.

We seek degreed professional with 5
or more years management experience in
internal communications. Must be skilled
in the publication of employee newsletters
as well as multi-media used for effective
internal communications. Strong
interpersonal and communications skills
are an absolute requirement.

Qualified candidates please forward
complete resume to:

Employment Manager
FIRST CHICAGO BANK
200 Lakeshore Drive
Chicago, IL 18374

An Equal Opportunity Employer

MELODY A. WAINSRIGHT

125 Sharon Circle   Home: (316) 924-3145
Hampstead, IL 18275   Office: (316) 337-9525

_____

July 14, 1997

Employment Manager
First Chicago Bank
200 Lakeshore Drive
Chicago, IL 18374

Dear Sir/Madam:

The position of Communications Manager, as advertised in this past Sunday's
edition of the *Chicago Tribune*, sounds like an exciting opportunity. Please
consider the enclosed resume an indication of my strong interest in this
position.

It appears that my qualifications are an excellent match for your
requirements.

Your advertisement calls for a degreed professional with 5 or more years
management experience in internal communications. My B.A. degree in English
and current position as Corporate Communications Manager for Worldwide
Insurance Company should meet your expectations.

Further, your ad states that you desire someone who is skilled in the
publication of employee newsletters as well as multi-media used for
effective communications. I now manage the publication of a corporate
monthly employee newsletter and 3 regional employee publications as well.
My use of muti-media for internal communications covers the gamut: overhead
transparencies, slides, audio casettes, VCR's, closed circuit TV, satellite
transmission, etc.

Both my interpersonal and communications skills are excellent, and have
always been a major area of strength for me.

Your opening sounds very interesting to me, and I would welcome the
opportunity to learn more during a personal interview at your offices. I
hope that you will view my candidacy favorably, and that I might have the
opportunity to further explore your requirements.

Thank you for your consideration, and I will look forward to hearing from
you.

Sincerely,

Melody A. Wainsright

Melody A. Wainsright

Enclosure

CORPORATE PLANNING

ANALYST

A key member of the Corporate Planning Team, the Corporate Planning Analyst will support the Vice President of Planning and members of the Company's senior management team in the identification, evaluation and selection of appropriate business strategies for maximizing short-term profits and long-term growth.

We seek an MBA with strong quantitative and analytical skills who thrives on financial "what if" analysis of business alternatives. In addition to analytical skills, the successful candidate will be capable of identifying/defining viable options that maximize profit potential of the firm. Exceptional communications and strong interpersonal skills are a must.

Our client is a Blue Chip leader in the petrochemical industry and offers outstanding opportunities for growth into general management.

For consideration, submit complete resume and salary requirements in strictest confidence to:

Mr. J. Walter Maltoon
Vice President
Search Consultants, Ltd
250 Park Avenue
New York, NY 19827

Executive Search Consultants

MARSHALL T. WENTWORTH
825 North Coventry Lane
Warren, NJ 17263

August 21, 1996

Mr. J. Walter Maltoon
Vice President
Search Consultants, Ltd.
250 Park Avenue
New York, NY 19827

Dear Mr. Maltoon:

While browsing through the *New York Times* this past Sunday, I came across your advertisement for a Corporate Planning Analyst. Although I am not actively "on the market," this position appears quite interesting and has prompted me to forward my resume for your review and consideration.

Review of your client's requirements, as specified in this advertisement, seems to suggest that I should be a very viable candidate for this opportunity. Please consider the following:

- MBA, Wharton School, University of Pennsylvania

- 3 Years as Business Analyst, General Foods Corporation

- Undergraduate Degree in Statistics With an Economics
  Minor

- Performed Numerous Studies and Made Best Recommendation
  on Various Business Strategies (e.g., buy, sell, merge,
  expand, contract, diversify, specialize, etc.).

My creativity and resourcefulness in identifying and presenting alternate business options has won the confidence and trust of the senior management team, and I am frequently chosen as the Lead Analyst on major project assignments. Interpersonal and communications skills are two of my major assets.

If you agree that I am well-qualified for this important position with your client, I would welcome the chance to meet with you to further explore this opportunity.

Since this is a confidential inquiry, I would much prefer being contacted at my home in the evening rather than at my office.

I appreciate your consideration, and look forward to hearing from you at your convenience. Thank you.

Sincerely,

Marshall T. Wentworth

Marshall T. Wentworth

Enclosure

CORPORATE PLANNING
MANAGER

A Fortune 500, internationally-known soup company with annual sales of $4.2 billion, we are in search of a top-flight manager for our Corporate Planning function.

This position reports to the Chief Financial Officer, and manages a staff of 20 high-powered analysts. Works directly with members of the Executive Committee in the development of viable business plans and strategies designed to maximize use of corporate resources and ROI.

We seek a Financial MBA with 10+ years business planning experience in a consumer products or process industry company. Must have successfully managed a team of business analysts and demonstrated the ability to formulate highly successful business strategies as measured in terms of financial results.

For consideration, please direct your complete resume with compensation requirements to:

Director of Corporate Employment

CAMPBELL SOUP COMPANY
Campbell Plaza
Camden, NJ 18273

An Equal Opportunity Employer

CAROL SUE REMLEY

18 Creek Road, West Chester, PA 19384

March 12, 1997

Director of Corporate Employment
Campbell Soup Company
Campbell Plaza
Camden, NJ 18273

Dear Sir/Madam:

I noted your ad for a Corporate Planning Manager in the March 11th edition of *The Philadelphia Inquirer* with considerable interest. This sounds like an excellent opportunity, and I would appear to have the qualifications you seek.

Enclosed is my resume for your consideration.

I am a Financial MBA with over 15 years experience in business planning. Currently, as Business Development and Planning Manager for Best Foods, a $1.3 billion frozen foods manufacturer, I manage a department of five talented analysts responsible for all business development and planning activities for the corporation.

Our overall charter is to develop and recommend those business plans and strategies required to effectively manage the resources of the business and maximize return on the firm's capital investment. Some key results achieved include:

- Diversification into the frozen juice market through acquisition of 2 key companies (Results = 20% ROI in second year)

- Consolidation of Fresh Cut and Greens Divisions into single business (Results = $30 million annual overhead savings)

- Business expansion into Pacific Rim (Results = 60% annual growth rate with excellent profitability)

- Sale of Guerner Dairy Products Division (Results = immediate improvement of 10% to corporate profits)

I have long admired Campbell Soup Company and would greatly appreciate the opportunity to be considered for this position. I feel that I am well prepared to take on this assignment, and have the knowledge, skills and energy to make a significant contribution to your company.

I would welcome the chance to meet with you and the members of your senior management group for the purpose of further exploring the specifics of your requirements. I look forward to hearing from you shortly. Thank you.

Sincerely,

Carol Sue Remley

Carol Sue Remley

Enclosure

JOEL R. GOLDBERG
126 West Curry Drive
Atlanta, GA 17263

March 29, 1995

Ms. Linda R. Sandstrom
Manager of Admin. Employment
North American Pharmaceutical, Inc.
10 Freedom Plaza
Valley Forge, PA 19116

Dear Ms. Sandstrom:

When opening the current issue of *Patent News* I accidentally spotted your advertisement for the position of Patent Attorney. Although I have not been looking for a change, your ad did catch my attention. I would very much like to work in the pharmaceutical industry, and your firm is particularly attractive to me.

My credentials, as called for in your ad, include a B.S. in Chemistry from Cornell University and over 2 years in the chemical industry as a Patent Attorney. My law degree is from Georgetown University School of Law.

I am currently working in the Corporate Law Division of Wilson Chemical Company, where I am their principal attorney in the patent area. Wilson, as you may know, is small, $30 million manufacturer of intermediate chemicals sold primarily to the pharmaceutical industry. As such, I have had to learn a good deal about pharmaceutical manufacturing processes.

I feel my qualifications are an excellent match for your requirements, and I would appreciate the opportunity to met with you and the members of your Law Staff to further discuss your requirements.

Thank you for your consideration. I look forward to hearing from you shortly.

Sincerely,

Joel R. Goldberg

Joel R. Goldberg

Enclosure

SENIOR VICE PRESENT

AND

GENERAL COUNSEL

Leading manufacturer of consumer products seeks heavily-seasoned attorney for the position of Senior Vice President and General Counsel. This position reports to the Chairman of the Board and directs a 40 employee Corporate Legal Department.

Successful candidate will have a minimum of 20 years experience in the corporate law division of a major manufacturing company. Must have a broad knowledge of corporate law to include both business and patent law. Must demonstrate solid track record in the successful management of cases involving multi-million dollar litigation across a wide range of legal issues.

Strong leadership and broad executive management capability are prerequisites. Excellent interpersonal and communications skills are also paramount.

Interested parties should forward complete resume and compensation requirements to:

Box Y–1172
THE WALL STREET JOURNAL
200 Park Avenue
New York NY 10887

An Equal Opportunity Employer

135 Russell Road
Wilton, CT 17294

November 12, 1996

Box Y-1172
Wall Street Journal
200 Park Avenue
New York, NY 10887

Dear Sir/Madam:

I was pleasantly surprised this morning to discover your advertisement for a Senior Vice President and General Counsel in the *Wall Street Journal* for two reasons. First, I have recently decided to make a career move. Second, I would appear to be well-suited to your requirements.

As Assistant General Counsel for Bristol Myers-Squibb, a $6 billion pharmaceutical and consumer products company, I report to the General Counsel and have managerial accountability for approximately half the Law Division (30 attorneys). For the last five years, my principal accountability has been to investigate and direct all major litigation work (several cases in the multi-million dollar range) covering a wide range of legal issues from antitrust cases, to consumer liability issues, to class action suits, to patent infringement suits, etc. I am proud to say that I have established a strong "winning" record over the years.

Interesting, as called for in your ad, I have broad knowledge of corporate law to include both general business and patent law. My career includes 5 years in the patent area, 3 years as a legal specialist in human relations, and 4 years in real estate related areas. This experience, coupled with my litigation background, should make me a very desirable candidate for the position you are attempting to fill.

My resume is enclosed for your consideration. As requested, my compensation requirements include a base salary in the $175,000 to $200,000 range plus executive bonus.

Should you conclude that I am a viable candidate for this position, I would be pleased to meet with you and the senior member of your management team to further explore my qualifications at your convenience.

Thank you for your consideration, and I look forward to your reply.

Sincerely,

William J. Feagles

William J. Feagles

WJF/jb

Enclosure

QUALITY MANAGER

We are a $220 million manufacturer of copper tubing sold to commercial developers and industrial OEM accounts.

We are in search of a Quality Manager for our copper refining and tube manufacturing facility located in Reading, Pennsylvania. This position reports to the Director of Operations and is responsible for managing the quality function for this 300 employee facility. Reporting to this position are 3 Quality Shift Supervisors and 2 Quality Laboratory Technicians.

The candidate we seek will have at least an Associates degree in science (Engineering Technology, Physics or Chemistry) and a minimum of 5 years quality supervisory/ management experience in the metals refining/finishing industry. Must have experience working with engineering and operations personnel to establish the quality standards, inspection and laboratory testing procedures necessary to meet industry standards and customer specifications.

Qualified candidates are encouraged to submit resume and salary requirements to:

Personnel Director
READING TUBE CORPORATION
200 Front Street
Reading, PA 19315

BARBARA COATES

305 North Church Street   Home: (908) 665-9038
East Orange, NJ 16284   Office:(908) 335-7171

                                        June 22, 1995

Personnel Director
Reading Tube Corporation
200 Front Street
Reading, PA 19315

Dear Sir/Madam:

This morning's *Reading Eagle* contained your advertisement for a Quality
Manager, a position in which I would be very interested. Enclosed you will
find a copy of my resume, therefore, for review and consideration.

Your ad states that you seek at least an Associates degree in science and a
minimum of 5 years quality supervisory or management experience in the
metals refining/finishing industry. My qualifications are:

  - B.S., Metallurgy, Colorado School of Mines

  - 6 Years Quality Experience, Revere Copper & Brass Co.

        2 Years - Manager of Quality Assurance
        4 Years - Quality Shift Supervisor

Further, as specified in your advertisement, the candidate must have
experience working with engineering and operations personnel to establish
the quality standards and inspection/laboratory test procedures to meet
industry standards and customer specifications. My qualifications include:

  - Extensive Experience Working with Engineering and
    Operations Personnel in All Areas Related to Quality

  - Publication of Quality Inspection and Testing Manual
    and Training of All Quality and Operations Personnel
    in Proper Inspection and Testing Methods

Hopefully, you will agree that I am well-qualified for your opening, and
that I will have the opportunity to further explore this position during a
face-to-face interview at your facility. I would welcome this opportunity
to discuss your requirements in greater detail.

Thank you for your consideration, and I look forward to your reply.

                                        Sincerely,

                                        Barbara Coates

                                        Barbara Coates

Enclosure

DIRECTOR

TOTAL QUALITY MANAGEMENT

Leading manufacturer of quality men's shoes seeks corporate Director of Total Quality Management. Position reports directly to the President.

This position will lead the design and implementation of a corporate-wide total quality effort based upon the principles and beliefs of Dr. Edwards Deming.

Seek Ph.D. in Statistics with 10+ years experience in total quality field. Must have been key architect and facilitator of a major SPC-based quality initiative in a multi- plant manufacturing company.

In addition to technical skills, must exhibit strong interpersonal, communications and leadership skills. Must be able to effectively relate to wide range of people, from top management to hourly operator.

Highly competitive salary, performance bonus, and comprehensive benefits program are provided.

Send resume, including compensation requirements, to:

Mr. David R. Levy
Vice President Human Resources

NATURALCRAFT SHOES, INC.
125 Carpenter Street
Wyomissing, PA 19284

JEFFREY R. TEMPLE

818 General Howe Drive
West Chester, PA 19382

Home: (215) 696-4067
Office: (215) 431-1726

June 16, 1997

Mr. David R. Levy
Vice President Human Resources
Naturalcraft Shoes, Inc.
125 Carpenter Street
Wyomissing, PA 19284

Dear Mr. Levy:

The Classified Section of today's *Philadelphia Inquirer* contained your advertisement for a Director of Total Quality. My qualifications appear to be an excellent match for this position, so I am enclosing my resume for your consideration.

I hold a Ph.D. in Statistics from the University of Delaware and, as called for in your ad, my qualifications include over 10 years experience in the total quality field.

In my current position as Manager of Quality for the Phillips Company, a $100 million manufacturer of men's clothing, I have successfully facilitated and led the development of a company-wide SPC-based quality initiative. This included implementation at three of our manufacturing sites.

In addition to my technical skills, I am considered to have strong interpersonal, communications and leadership skills. All of these characteristics were prerequisites to entering my current position, and have been critical qualifications needed for effective performance. The success of our current effort provides ample testimony to my strengths in these important areas.

I am a strong Deming advocate, and get excited about the opportunity to assume a Director level position in a company looking for key leadership in implementing a corporate-wide total quality effort based upon his teachings. I feel I have much to bring to Naturalcraft Shoes as a candidate, and could well have the overall knowledge and capability necessary to successfully leading your total quality effort.

I would encourage your strong consideration of my employment candidacy, and would hope that we would have the opportunity to meet shortly.

Thank you for your consideration, and I look forward to hearing from you.

Very truly yours,

Jeffrey R. Temple

Jeffrey R. Temple

Enclosure

MANUFACTURING MANAGER

American Foam, Inc. is a $20 million manufacturer of reticulated and unreticulated polyurethane foam sold to acoustical and filtration applications. We have experienced excellent growth and increased profitability over the last 5 years, and are planning a $5 million capital expansion this year.

We seek a talented, seasoned Manufacturing Manager for our 2 plant, 110 employee operation. This position reports to the Executive Vice President and will manage a staff of 12 Manufacturing Shift Superviors.

The successful candidate will hold a degree in Engineering (prefer Ch.E.) and at least 8 to 10 years management experience in the manufacture of polyurethane foam or other polymer-based products. Desire excellent interpersonal, communications and leadership skills. Prefer some prior plant start-up experience.

Excellent compensation and benefits package is provided.

For consideration, please forward complete resume and recent salary history to:

Manager of Human Resources
AMERICAN FOAM, INC.
240 Old River Road
Richmond, VA 13948

An Equal Opportunity Employer M/F

JEANNE FOX

205 Street Road   Home: (216) 844-1284
Cleveland, OH 12847   Office:(216) 775-0987

August 21, 1994

Manager of Human Resources
American Foam, Inc.
240 Old River Road
Richmond, VA 13948

Dear Sir/Madam:

The position of Manufacturing Manager, as advertised in the August 20th edition of the *Cleveland Plain Dealer*, is a surprisingly good match for my qualifications!

Consider the following:

- B.S. Chemical Engineering, Virginia Polytechnical Institute

- 15 Years Manufacturing Experience - Polyurethane Foam

- Start-Up Experience as Plant Manager - Philadelphia Plant

- Excellent interpersonal, communications and leadership skills

In my current position as Manufacturing Manager for Johnson Foams, Inc., I manage an $18 million, 3 plant, 75 employee operation engaged in the manufacture of specialty polyurethane foams. During the last 3 years in this position, key accomplishments have included:

- Reduction in Operating Costs of 20% (Annual Savings of $2 million)

- Increased Production Throughput by 10% (Annual Value of $1.2 Million)

- Reduced Staff by 5% (Annual Saving of $1/2 million)

Perhaps I could make similar contributions to your firm.

I would appreciate the opportunity to meet with you and appropriate members of your executive team to further explore your requirements and my qualifications.

I look forward to your reply, and hope that we will have the opportunity to meet in the near future. Thank you for your consideration.

Sincerely,

Jeanne Fox

Jeanne Fox

Enclosure

DIRECTOR OF MANUFACTURING

The Agricultural Products Division of our $3.8 billion, Delaware-based chemical company is looking for a talented Director of Manufacturing for its 6 plant, 2,400 employee chemical manufacturing operation. This position reports to the Division President.

We seek a B.S. Ch.E. with 20+ years manufacturing experience in agricultural or specialty chemicals. Must demonstrate strong performance record in the profitable management of a sizeable, complex, multi-plant operation. Must also exhibit strong working knowledge of modern manufacturing concepts, to include: JIT, MRP, SPC-based total quality and employee empowerment.

Conversion of culture from "top down" management approach to a sociotechnical systems-based operation will require appropriate management style conducive to successful leadership of this cultural shift.

Interested candidates should forward resume and compensation requirements to:

Mr. John Dawson
Vice President Operations
NATIONAL CHEMICALS, INC.
325 East DuPont Blvd.
Wilmington, DL 18273

Equal Opportunity Employer, M/F

BARRY R. REMLEY
125 Pine Cone Lane
Wilmington, NC 17263

September 16, 1996

Mr. John Dawson
Vice President Operations
National Chemicals, Inc.
325 East DuPont Blvd.
Wilmington, DL 18273

Dear Mr. Dawson:

If, as your September 16th ad in the *Wilmington News* suggests, you are looking for a top flight executive to lead your manufacturing function, you may want to give my credentials careful consideration. I appear to be an excellent match for your current requirements.

Please consider the following relevant highlights of my qualifications:

- B.S. Chemical Engineering, North Carolina State University.

- 26 Years Total Chemicals Manufacturing Experience (8 Years Agricultural Chemicals)

- Management of a $2.6 billion, 4 Plant, 1,600 Employee, Specialty Chemicals Operation

- First-Hand Experience with Modern Manufacturing Concepts/Approaches Including: JIT, MRP, SPC-Based Total Quality, etc.

- Extensive Training In, and Experience With, Socio-Technical Systems Approach to Management (Implemented Across All Operations)

- Strong History of Successful Financial Performance

The enclosed resume will provide you with the specifics of my manufacturing management experience and accomplishments.

Should you agree that I am a strong candidate for your requirements, I would welcome the opportunity to meet with you personally to explore the possible contributions that I can make to National Chemicals, Inc.

My compensation requirements are a base salary in the $125K to $135K range plus bonus.

Thank you for your consideration.

Sincerely,

Barry R. Remley

Barry R. Remley

Enclosure

GENERAL MANAGER

We are part of a division of a world-wide supplier of technology, products and services for the energy market. Currently, we have unprecedented opportunity for growth and are searching for a General Manager to direct the operation of our two manufacturing facilities in Southern Indiana.

This highly visible position will be filled by a candidate who has a proven track record in managing manufacturing operations at the $100 to $150 million level and who will have repeatedly demonstrated the ability to cost effectively increase velocity and throughput in operations. Position requires a degree in engineering or business, a solid record of accomplishment in increasingly responsible positions in a manufacturing environment, and excellent communications skills.

Qualified candidates are encouraged to send their resume and salary history in confidence to:

**Box 222–D
THE CHICAGO TRIBUNE
Chicago, IL 17384**

OTTO W. RENNER III

125 East Brook Road, Arlington, TX 18725

April 13, 1995

Box 222-D
The Chicago Tribune
Chicago, IL 17384

Dear Sir/Madam:

Today's *Chicago Tribune* contains your advertisement for a General Manager, along with a brief description of the requirements for this position. My background appears to satisfy your requirements rather well, so I am enclosing my resume for your review and consideration.

I am currently Group Manufacturing Manager for a $115 million, 3 plant division of Charman Manufacturing, a leader in the field of precision specialty gauges for the nuclear power industry. I hold a dual degree in Mechanical and Electrical Engineering at the bachelor's level.

Evidence of ability to be a solid contributor to business results includes:

- Increased production output by 28% through redesign of manufacturing equipment layout (annual value of $8.6 million)

- Decreased manufacturing costs by 21% over 3 years through reduction in manpower, improved inventory planning and manufacturing scheduling, and reduction in spare parts inventory ($6.3 million annual savings)

- Implemented total quality program resulting in 96% reduction in scrap and a 98% reduction in customer complaints ($1.4 million annual savings)

These are but a few of the key results I have achieved on behalf of my employers throughout my career in manufacturing. Additional achievements are detailed in the enclosed resume.

As my resume will confirm, I have experienced excellent career progression and have advanced rather rapidly to positions of increasing responsibility in the manufacturing field. Additionally, I am credited with having strong communications and leadership skills.

My current annual compensation is $115,000. This includes a base salary of $95,000 plus a bonus of $20,000.

I would welcome the opportunity to meet with you for the purpose of exploring the contributions that I could make to your company.

Thank you for your consideration, and I look forward to your reply.

Sincerely,

Otto W. Renner III

Otto W. Renner III

Enclosure

PRESIDENT & CEO

Internationally known, East Coast-based environmental engineering company seeks senior executive to head up $180 million firm. Position reports to the Chairman and will have considerable latitude in the day-to-day management of this high growth company.

Successful candidates will possess a degree in engineering, an MBA and at least 10 years senior management experience in a technology-based consulting firm. Must have demonstrated leadership skills in a fast growth environment and an excellent track record of profitably growing new businesses through both acquisition and development of new consulting services.

Base salary in the upper $100K range, plus highly attractive bonus program, car, and other executive perks in keeping with this level position.

For consideration, please forward your resume in confidence to:

**Box 412–C
THE BOSTON GLOBE
Boston, MA 18293**

LEE W. KRUG

136 Breakers Way
Ocean Beach, CA 16284

Home: (912) 875-9090
Office: (912) 227-3131

July 16, 1997

Box 412-C
The Boston Globe
Boston, MA 18293

Dear Sir/Madam:

Your July 16th *Boston Globe* advertisement for a President & CEO reads like a carbon copy of my credentials. Perhaps we should meet to discuss the possibilities for a successful relationship.

Please consider the following qualifications as they relate to your needs:

- M.S. Environmental Engineering, B.S. Chemical Engineering

- MBA, Finance, Columbia University,

- 20 years total experience - technical consulting
  10 years experience - environmental consulting
  8 years senior management - $120 million firm

- Managed rapid-growth business units expanding at annual growth rate of 45%+

- Heavily involved in leading business growth through both acquisition and new business development

In my current position as Executive Vice President of Enviro-Tech, a $130 million environmental engineering consulting firm, I am responsible to the President for the daily operating results of the firm's 6 consulting divisions. I am also a member of the Senior Executive Committee, and am considered to be a key force in formulation of both long and short-range business strategy.

May I suggest that we meet to further discuss your requirements? I believe that I am uniquely suited to your requirements and have the knowledge and leadership skills necessary to successfully lead your business.

I look forward to hearing from you shortly.

Thank you.

Sincerely,

Lee W. Krug
Lee W. Krug

Enclosure

5

Networking Cover Letters

No good book on cover letters could possibly be complete without a thorough chapter on the subject of the networking cover letter.

There have been several studies that measure the effectiveness of various job-hunting sources. All agree on one thing—employment networking, by far, is the single most productive source for finding jobs! In fact, various studies have shown that somewhere between 63 and 75 percent of all jobs are actually found through use of the networking process.

WHAT IS EMPLOYMENT NETWORKING?

Employment networking is the process by which the job seeker makes use of his or her personal contacts to find employment. The idea is to make use of your personal contacts to arrange introductions to others who could be influential in helping you with your job search.

The networking process, in principle, works much like the popular chain-letter concept (or cell division theory). It allows you to exponentially expand your own personal contacts by tapping into the social network of others. The process looks something like this:

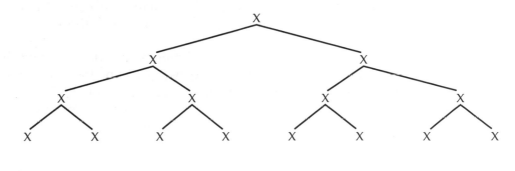

If each contact you make in the chain leads to only two other contacts, as you can see from the above example, two initial contacts can quickly multiply to eight contacts. Thus, by asking each contact to introduce you to two or three other persons who might help you with advice or assistance in your job search, it is quite possible to eventually solicit the advice and help of several hundred other persons who become actively involved in some way with your job search. This is an extremely powerful force and a job-hunting technique that has demonstrated its effectiveness time and time again!

It is not our purpose here, however, to train you in use of the networking process. If you need help in this area, let me suggest that you refer to one of my other books, *Get the Right Job in 60 Days or Less* (Wiley), which provides over 180 pages on the specifics of how to effectively use the networking process as a key tool in your job search. Instead, it is the purpose of this chapter to assist you with the composition of effective networking cover letters that can help to facilitate the effectiveness of the employment networking approach.

PURPOSE OF NETWORKING COVER LETTER

Essentially, the purpose of the networking cover letter is threefold:

1. Set the stage for a personal introduction
2. Transmit your resume
3. Acquaint the person with your qualifications in advance of your networking contact (that is, phone call or meeting)

This then becomes an important document in helping the networking process to flow properly. A well-designed, well-written cover letter will go a long way toward setting the stage for your networking contact. If well done, the letter will accomplish the following:

1. Make the person whom you are contacting feel comfortable—willing to open up and share valuable information (that is, job leads and names of key contacts) with you.
2. Provide sufficient information about your qualifications and job-search objectives to allow the contact to make intelligent recommendations to you.
3. Provide sufficient information to allow the contact to intelligently discuss your qualifications and job interests with others.

Conversely, should the cover letter be poorly-designed or poorly-written, most (if not all) of these potential benefits will be lost and your targeted contact will not be in a position to provide meaningful help.

So, it should be obvious that a well-written networking cover letter is critical to the success of your job-hunting campaign.

ELEMENTS OF NETWORKING COVER LETTER

The following is a summary of the basic elements of a well-written networking cover letter:

1. Personalized opening paragraph to include:
   a. Name of the person who has referred you
   b. Nature of your relationship with this person
   c. Some personal comments (where appropriate)
2. Explanation of how referral came about (optional)
3. Reason for job/career change (optional)
4. Reference to known job opening (if one exists)
5. Indirect networking approach (if no known job exists)
6. Brief overall summary of qualifications (and reference to enclosed resume)
7. Action statement—designed to initiate next action, with contact information (that is, phone call or personal meeting)
8. Statement of appreciation (thank you)

The cover letter samples that comprise the rest of this chapter should provide you with an ample array of models from which to choose in tailoring your own networking cover letters.

WILLIAM C. CHAMBERS
125 Woods Lane
Wilbraham, MA 13975

October 15, 1996

Mr. David R. Lansberry
National Sales Manager
Westclock Corporation
2015 Yorkshire Highway
Springfield, MA 13977

Dear David:

John Thompson mentioned your name to me the other day,
and strongly suggested I contact you. John and I grew up
together in Flint, Michigan and still see one another
frequently.

From what John tells me, you are very active as an
officer in the National Hardware Marketing Association
and know a number of sales executives in the industry. As
a result, he felt you might be willing to lend me a hand.

National Hardware, my current employer, has recently been
sold to Servicestar Corporation. Servicestar has its own
sales organization, and will simply fold National
Hardware's product line into their existing line.
Unfortunately this means that my job, along with the jobs
of 25 other Sales Representatives, has been eliminated.

As the enclosed resume shows, I have a B.A. degree in
Marketing from Ohio State, and have been working as a
Sales Representative in the hardware industry for 2
years.

Although I certainly would not expect you to be aware of
a specific job opportunity for me, I would appreciate if
you could spend an hour or so with me over lunch. I would
value any general thoughts and advice you might have
concerning my job hunting campaign. John seemed to
feel you might be very helpful in this regard.

I will plan to call you next Monday to see when it might
be convenient for us to meet. I would very much
appreciate your counsel.

Thank you.

Sincerely,

Bill Chambers

William C. Chambers

Enclosure

136 West Terrace Lane
Nashville, TN 13748

August 15 1995

Ms. Katherine B. Oliver
Executive Director
American Marketing Association
335 Park Avenue
New York, NY 16284

Dear Ms. Oliver:

As the chief executive officer of the nation's largest professional marketing association, I felt you might be in a position to provide some excellent counsel and advice. I have been an Association member since 1986, and have been active on various regional committees. You may recall, we met briefly over lunch at last year's national meeting in Chicago.

I am currently Vice President of Sales for the Martin Corporation, a $1.5 billion manufacturer of electric motors sold to OEM accounts. In this capacity, I manage an international salesforce of over 150 employees and market our products in some 16 countries. A confidential copy of my resume is enclosed for your reference.

Although I have had quite a successful career to-date, some recent top management changes at Martin have caused me to rethink my objectives. As a result, I have decided to make a change and am currently conducting a highly confidential job search. Martin is unaware of my decision.

I would appreciate if you could spend a few minutes with me on the phone sometime in the next few days. I would value your observations and insight concerning current national trends in the sales profession and how these might impact my job search. Additionally, I would welcome any general thoughts and ideas that you might have regarding my search.

I will plan to call you shortly, and look forward to our conversation. In the meantime, I would appreciate any thought that you might give to this matter.

Thank you.

Very truly yours,

Marcia T. Renner

Marcia T. Renner

Enclosure

DONALD C. LAWLER

135 White Cap Road   Home: (313) 975-2284
Ocean Park, CA 15385   Office:(313) 336-9595

                                                     March 22, 1997

Mr. Robert T. Baker
Brand Manager
General Foods Corporation
1200 Corporate Blvd.
White Plains, NY 16283

Dear Bob:

I am writing to you at the suggestion of Ray Walden, who I understand is a
former neighbor of yours. Ray and I were fraternity brothers at Arizona
State, and have stayed in touch over the years.

The other night, over dinner, Ray and I were discussing my plans for a
career change and your name came up as someone who has a strong
professional network in the consumer marketing field. Ray felt, as a
result, you might be in a position to lend me a hand.

Bob, don't get me wrong. I am not expecting that you would have a job for
me, nor would I expect that you would be aware of one. Instead, what I am
hoping is that you might be willing to share the names of a few good
contacts in the consumer marketing field -- persons, like you, who are
professionally active and know others in the field. I would also appreciate
any general suggestions you might have concerning my job hunting campaign.

I have taken the liberty of enclosing my resume for your reference. In
short, I have a B.A. in Business from Arizona State and 3 years experience
as a Market Analyst with Armstrong World Industries. I am seeking a similar
position with a major consumer products company on the East Coast.

Bob, I will plan to give you a call sometime during the next week, and
would hope that you will be able to spend a few minutes with me. I would
greatly appreciate your advice and counsel.

Thank you.

                                                     Sincerely,

                                                     Don Lawler

                                                     Donald C. Lawler

DCL/em

Enclosure

MARY F. BURGOON

325 East River Blvd.
Harrisburg, PA 19284

Home: (717) 355-8176
Office: (717) 234-1948

February 22, 1995

Mr. John A. Stapleton
President
Stapleton Industries
1345 Market Street
Philadelphia, PA 19117

Dear Mr. Stapleton:

Harrry Williams, a tennis partner and friend, thought it would be a good idea for me to contact you. Harry and I have been playing doubles together at Hershey Tennis Club for the last 5 years, and also serve on the Board of Directors of Green Valley Country Club. I understand, from Harry, that you're quite a tennis player yourself. He tells me that the last time the two of you met on the courts you thoroughly humiliated him with your power serve.

During tennis last week, I mentioned to Harry that I would be leaving my position as Director of Marketing for General Precision. General Precision, as you know, is a leading manufacturer of specialty control instrumentation for the chemical process industry.

As President of a major player in the process control field, Harry seemed to feel you would be an excellent person to talk with about my career change. He tells me that you are a very knowledgeable guy and might have some good advice that would be helpful to my job search. I would very much value your counsel in this regard.

I have enclosed a copy of my resume to facilitate our discussion, and would appreciate if you might have a moment to look it over.

Knowing that you likely have a busy schedule, I will contact your secretary early next week to see if we can establish a convenient time for us to talk. I look forward to our conversation, and would very much appreciate your advice and counsel.

Thank you.

Sincerely,

Mary F. Burgoon

MFB/dm

Enclosure

WILLARD R. SMITH

126 New Market Street   Home: (818) 335-1928
Canton, Ohio 17247   Office:(818) 495-8874

July 28, 1996

Robert J. Bastin
Director of Manufacturing
Miller Brewing Company
Milwaukee, WI 17365

Dear Mr. Bastin:

When searching through the *Sigma Chi Alumni Directory*, I cam across your name. (I am a 1993 graduate of the University of Wisconsin, where I was Vice President of the local Sigma Chi Chapter). I am writing in hopes that you might be in a position to provide me with some advice and assistance.

I have recently elected to make a career change, and am looking to find a new position in manufacturing in the food and/or beverage industry. Since graduating with a B.S. in Industrial Engineering in 1993, I have been in manufacturing with Pepsi Cola Bottling Company. Most recently, I have been Operations Manager for a 150 employee bottling operation here in the Canton area.

Although Pepsi has been good to me, and I have learned a good deal in the 3 years since graduation, I do miss the Wisconsin area. Both my wife and I are from the Greater Milwaukee area and would love to return, provided I am able to find a comparable position to the position I now hold at Pepsi.

Mr. Bastin, as a member of Sigma Chi and as a manufacturing executive with a major beverage company in the Milwaukee area, I thought you might be a good person to contact. Although it is unlikely that Miller Brewing would coincidentally be looking for someone with my background, I thought perhaps you might be in a position to introduce me to other manufacturing executives in the Milwaukee area through whom I might network in finding a suitable opening. In addition, I would greatly appreciate any suggestions you might personally have concerning my job search.

I have taken the liberty of enclosing my resume for your reference.

I would very much appreciate if you could spare a few minutes with me on the phone to discuss this matter. Your help would be greatly appreciated.

I will plan to call your Secretary to see if I can coordinate a time that would be convenient to your schedule.

Thank you very much for your assistance in this matter, and I look forward to talking with you.

Sincerely,

Willard R Smith

Willard R. Smith

Enclosure

MARTHA T. LUDWIG
825 Green Tree Lane
Birmingham, AL 24375

February 23, 1995

Mr. Walter Creighton
Vice President of Manufacturing
Reardon Industries, Inc.
825 Industry Highway, NE
Atlanta, GA 13296

Dear Walter:

I am writing to you as a fellow member of the American Manufacturers' Association to request your assistance and advice concerning a career change that I am planning. You may recall, we were introduced by Ann Johnson at the last AMA meeting in Boston, and talked at length about implementation of TQC at the operating level. I enjoyed our conversation very much.

Currently, I am Vice President of Operations for Birmingham Industries, Inc., a $350 million manufacturer of industrial valves. Although a fine company, unfortunately Birmingham is family-owned and literally all senior management personnel are members of the Lawler family. This does not bode well for long-term career growth, so I have quietly opted to pursue a career search to find an environment that offers brighter long-term growth prospects.

Walter, although I am not expecting that you will be aware of a specific opening for me, I would very much appreciate the opportunity to talk with you more broadly about my job search campaign. I would certainly value your observations about the general market as well as any ideas you might have that would be helpful to my job hunting approach.

I am enclosing my resume for your review, and will plan to give you a call shortly.

By the way, Ann was aware that I would be contacting you and said to say "hello". She mentioned that she was planning to look you up at the AMA meeting next month in San Diego, and has some interesting information for you concerning the problem you were having with SPC training of operating personnel.

Walter, I greatly appreciate your help concerning my job search and look forward to our discussion.

Thank you.

Very truly yours,

Martha Ludwig

Martha T. Ludwig

MTL/sk

Enclosure

DAVID S. CHEN

626 Cliff Top Road, Albany, NY 13465

August 15, 1996

Ms. Linda R. Loften
Engineering Manager
Westinghouse Corporation
800 East Commerce Street
Pittsburgh, PA 14274

Dear Ms. Loften:

Sheri Foster, one of my associates here at General Electric, suggested that I contact you. Sheri and I have jointly worked on various engineering projects here at G.E.'s Albany small motors plant, and have gotten to know each other quite well. She tells that she had worked two summers for you as a Co-op student while attending the University of Michigan.

Ms. Loften, after considerable soul-searching, I have decided to make a career change. I have spent the last two years, since earning my engineering degree from the University of Michigan, working as a Design Engineer on small motors. Quite frankly, I have not found this work particularly interesting, and would much prefer working in the energy-related field on larger equipment such as industrial boilers, heat exchangers, etc.

Sheri tells me you direct an engineering department responsible for design of large boilers and pressure vessels. It is for this reason that she has suggested I contact you.

Although you may not have an opening at Westinghouse for someone with my credentials, both Sheri and I felt you might have some ideas and suggestions on how to make the transition to the energy-related equipment field. I know, with two years experience in the design of small motors, this may not be an easy transition for me to make. I would therefore very much value your advice and counsel on this subject.

I have enclosed an informational copy of my resume for your review, and would like to give you a call sometime during the next week or so. Perhaps I could prearrange an appropriate time to call through your secretary.

I would sincerely appreciate your advice and counsel on this subject, and look forward to talking with you. I hope that your busy schedule will allow us to talk in the near future.

Thank you for your help in this matter.

Sincerely,

David S. Chen

David S. Chen

Enclosure

JUDITH M. RESISSER
1835 Weelstone Place
Rockford, IL 18274

January 15, 1997

Dr. Blandon F. Weinberg
Senior Vice President - Technology
American Foods Corporation
600 Industry Avenue, SW
Chicago, IL 16249

Dear Blandon:

John Thorton, a close friend of mine, suggested I contact you. John and I have adjoining slips at Safe Harbour Marina, where we have spent several summer weekends sailing together. I understand that you enjoy a bit of sailing as well.

Last weekend, while at Perskie Island, I mentioned to John that I had decided to make a career move. Since my background is in senior engineering management, John suggested that I might want to contact you to see if you have any thoughts on this matter.

As you can see from the enclosed resume, I have an M.S. in Chemical Engineering from North Carolina State and over 20 years engineering experience in the chemical process industry. Currently, I am Director of Engineering for Dow Chemical's Polymers Division, where I direct a 250 employee central engineering group concerned with the engineering design, installation and start-up of major polymer manufacturing facilities. A copy of my resume is enclosed, providing you with further details of my background.

As it turns out, Blandon, I will be in Chicago for two weeks starting January 20th. Perhaps, if your schedule would permit, we could meet over dinner. I would welcome the opportunity to discuss my job search with you, and would appreciate your general counsel and advice on this matter. I will call your office early next week to see if your schedule will allow us to get together.

Thank you for your help with this matter, Blandon, and I look forward to the possibility of meeting with you personally.

Very truly yours,

Judy Resisser

Judith M. Resisser

JMR/st

Enclosure

137 Laredo Street, SW
Houston, TX 12840

September 15, 1997

Dr. Adrian M. Mathers
Director of Absorbant Technology
Kimberly-Clark Corporation
Technology Center
800 Welseley Lane, SE
Atlanta, GA 15274

Dear Dr. Mathers:

Carlton Evers, a former member of your technical staff, has suggested I contact you. Carlton and I are colleagues and have worked together in the Product Development Group of Wellington Fibers Corporation for the last two years.

Dr. Mathers, Carlton has told me about some of the work that your group has been doing on the development of new super absorbant systems for use in the development of incontinence diapers. He thought my recent work involving the use of polymer-based gels for super absorbant applications may be of interest to your organization.

I have recently made a decision to leave Wellington Fibers, to seek employment in the Technology Department of a larger corporation, where there is greater emphasis on basic research. It would appear that my background could be an excellent fit with some of the areas on which you are working. I am therefore enclosing a copy of my resume for your review and consideration.

Perhaps, if you do not currently have an opening on your staff, you would be kind enough to share some of your general thoughts and ideas on others with whom I should be in contact in the field of absorbancy. I would sincerely welcome your advice and counsel in this regard.

I will plan to call your office this Monday, to arrange a convenient time for us to talk. I would greatly appreciate any assistance that you could provide to me regarding this matter.

Thank you very much.

Sincerely,

Joan F. Swanson

Joan F. Swanson

Enclosure

OLIVER R. STONE, PH.D.

605 Clearview Lane   Home: (818) 774-0937
Westville, NH 13749   Office:(818) 699-4047

June 23, 1994

Mr. William F. Baron, Jr.
President
Dutch Master Paints, Inc.
605 Wently Street
Boston, MA 17295

Dear Bill:

I am writing to you at the suggestion of Richard Smart, a close friend and former classmate of mine at Boston University. Dick and I were having lunch together last Wednesday, when I mentioned to him that I was planning to make a career change. He suggested that perhaps you might be an excellent person to contact concerning my plans, and mentioned that you have a lot of contacts in the paint and related industry areas.

Bill, I would doubt that you would be aware of a specific job opportunity for me, however, I would certainly appreciate the chance to talk with you about my job search in a more general sense. Dick tells me that you have been very active in various industry associations and, in your current capacity, stay very much on top of what is happening in the industry. Perhaps you would be kind enough to share some of your observations about current industry trends and events which might impact my job search. In any event, I would be most appreciative of any general thoughts and ideas you might have on this subject.

Enclosed please find a copy of my resume for your review. Briefly, I have a Ph.D. in Polymer Engineering from Cornell University and over 25 years research experience in the development of pigments and dyes sold to industrial applications. Most recently, I have been Vice President of Technology for Wilson Chemical Company, responsible for a 50 employee research department in the development of specialty dyes and pigments sold to the paint industry. I am sure you are familiar with our firm.

Bill, I would very much appreciate the opportunity to discuss this matter with you, and would sincerely welcome your insights concerning both the industry and my job search.

I will plan to give your office a call next week, and look forward to the opportunity to talk with you personally. Dick has told me a great deal about you.

Thank you for your willingness to be of assistance, and I look forward to our conversation.

Sincerely,

Oliver Stone

Oliver R. Stone

Enclosure

DEBORAH S. MORGAN

625 Shady Lane   Home: (317) 897-2837
Wilmington, DL 18246   Office: (317) 638-4921

October 14, 1997

Ms. Karen P Kleiner
Manager of Accounting
Darlington Manufacturing, Inc.
605 Barrington Road
West Point, NY 17395

Dear Karen:

I was taking with Sandy Duncan the other evening, and she suggested that I give you a call. Sandy and I have been very active in the local Chapter of National Business and Professional Women, and have done a lot of scheming together on ways that women might be more assertive in taking control of their careers, and not simply taking what is handed to them.

I guess that I have taken a lot of our conversations to heart, and have now decided that it is time to take charge of my own career. Unfortunately, I find myself in a very male-dominated environment here at Thornton, Smith and Kaufman, and will need to make a career move if I am going to expect to move ahead with both my career and professional development.

Thornton, Smith and Kaufman is a small but high quality CPA firm located here in Wilmington. They have an excellent reputation and a strong base of medium-sized manufacturing and service clients. I joined them as an Auditor in their Auditing Department two years ago, following receipt of my Accounting degree from the University of Delaware. A copy of my resume is enclosed for your reference.

Karen, I would like to make the transition from public accounting to a position in manufacturing cost accounting with a medium to large manufacturing company, where there would be reasonable expectation for career growth based upon contribution and performance. My current compensation is $32,000 annually.

As an accounting manager for a medium-sized manufacturing firm, Sandy seemed to feel you would be an excellent person for me to talk with on this matter. I understand that you successfully made a similar transition a couple of years ago yourself. As a result, you might be in a position to share some of your observations and insights.

I would really appreciate an opportunity to talk with you, and would sincerely welcome any overall suggestions that you might have regarding my career search. Perhaps I could call your secretary to arrange for a time that would be convenient to your schedule. Sandy has told me so much about you, and I really look forward to our conversation.

Thank you for your help, and I look forward to talking with you soon.

Sincerely,

Deborah Morgan

Deborah S. Morgan

Enclosure

JOYCE BUZINSKI

825 North Hill Road
Utica, NY 17296

Home: (315) 775-9076
Office:(315) 664-9025

May 16, 1994

Mr. Roderick P. Blake
Senior Partner
Coopers & Lyrandt
1225 Chestnut Street
Philadelphia, PA 19274

Dear Rod:

I can see by your new title that things are going rather well for you at C&L. Congratulations!

It hardly seems like yesterday that you and I were talking about your desire to make a move from manufacturing to the world of the Big 6. I guess the introduction that I arranged for you with Dave Smith was just the thing you needed to get your career really rolling. I'm glad that things have worked out so well. It's always refreshing to see talented people rise to the top!

Rod, I only wish that my own career was doing as well. Although I really can't complain about having finally "arrived", so to speak, as C.F.O. of SPF Industries, a recent change in the top management of the business has me concerned. As you know, Dave Thurmon has just been named President here at SPF. Although he is certainly a nice guy, I really don't believe he has the candle power to pull SPF out of the slide it is experiencing in recent years. As a result, I feel it is time to start actively thinking about a serious career move.

I was wondering what your schedule might look like for lunch sometime in the next week or so. I would really like to get together with you to see what ideas you might have concerning my job search. My decision is highly confidential, of course, and I'm going to need to be most discreet in how I go about doing this. I would really welcome your advice and counsel in this regard.

Why don't I give Sally a call to see what we can set up? I would really appreciate your help on this, and look forward to our conversation.

Thanks, Rod, and I look forward to seeing you.

Sincerely,

Joyce

Joyce Buzinski

P.S. I've enclosed a reference copy of my "draft" resume.

SAMUEL P. HARPER
305 Blue Canyon Drive
Boulder, CO 12225

August 29, 1996

Mr. William Courtney
Manager of Financial Planning
Wilton Corporation
200 Trader Avenue
Denver, CO 12238

Dear Bill:

It has been about 2 years since our last contact, but I'm sure you will remember the work that we did together on the proposed Frederick merger. At the time, as you will likely recall, I was working as the Senior Analyst for Beard Associates on the project.

Bill, unfortunately, the current recession has not been too kind to Beard Associates. There hasn't exactly been a plethora of merger and acquisition activity lately, and Beard has just announced its decision to cease operations effective October 15th. Thus, I am in search of a new career opportunity.

As you may remember, Bill, I hold an MBA from the Wharton School, where my major was Finance. I have been working as a financial analyst for Beard since June of 1993 (following graduation), principally focusing on providing technical support to client management in the financial evaluation of proposed M&A's. I have enclosed an informational copy of my resume to provide you with further details.

I am planning to be in the Denver area next week on business and was wondering if we might be able to meet. I would really appreciate some general advice and counsel concerning my job search, and thought perhaps we might do this over dinner, provided your schedule will permit. If not, maybe we can compare schedules and find a time that better fits your requirements.

Bill, I really enjoyed working with you on the Frederick project, and came to have a great deal of respect for your knowledge of corporate finance. I would very much value your advice and counsel concerning my career, and hope that your schedule will allow us to meet. I will call you later this week to see when we might get together.

Thanks, Bill, for your help in this matter, and I look forward to seeing you again.

Sincerely,

Sam Harper

Samuel P. Harper

SPH/cb

Enclosure

STUART A. SCHWARTZ

314 Valley View Drive, New Hartford, NY 16397

August 21, 1997

Mr. Phillip P. Thurmond
Chief Financial Officer
Xerox Corporation
200 Xerox Plaza
Rochester, NY 17284

Dear Mr. Thurmond:

Your name was given to me by Bill Parlett, President of the Greater Utica Chamber of Commerce. I understand that the two of you were neighbors and used to do a lot of sailing together when Bill lived in Rochester. Bill and I have worked together on several Chamber projects over the last 3 years, and have gotten to know one another quite well.

During last Wednesday's Chamber meeting, I mentioned to Bill that I was planning to make a career change. Since I have a strong background in finance, he seemed to feel that I should contact you, and suggested that I use his name in doing so.

As summarized on the enclosed resume, I hold an MBA in Finance from the University of Chicago. After nearly 20 years in the Corporate Finance Department of General Electric, I moved to the Utica area as Director of Corporate Finance for the Marlton Corporation, a $600 million manufacturer of computer components. This has not proven to be the opportunity initially painted by Marlton, and I have thus decided to return to the corporate financial world of the major corporation.

Although it is unlikely that you will be aware of a specific job opportunity for me, I would appreciate the opportunity to meet with you briefly to discuss my career plans and to benefit from any general advice and counsel that you might provide in this regard. It would also be valuable to get your insight concerning the state of the electronics/communications industry and the prospects for developing a fruitful career as a senior financial executive in this industry segment.

Realizing that you have a very busy schedule, I am fully prepared to adjust my own schedule accordingly. Perhaps, if convenient, we might even meet over an early breakfast. In any event, I will plan to call your secretary early next week to see if a convenient time might be worked out.

Mr. Thurmond, I really appreciate your help with my career search and look forward to the prospect of meeting with you personally. Thank you for your help in this matter.

Sincerely,

Stuart A. Schwartz

Stuart A. Schwartz

SAS/dr

Enclosure

LYNN E. NEMSER
124 Pleasant Grove Road
Pittsburgh, PA 16248

September 21, 1996

Mr. Karl F. Johnson
Manager of Human Resources
American Home Products Company
800 Prince Blvd.
Chicago, IL 17263

Dear Mr. Johnson:

You may recall that I was a Human Resources Intern in AHP's Corporate Benefits Department 2 years ago, while a senior at Michigan State University. I certainly appreciated the opportunity to have lunch with you during my internship, and valued your overall suggestions concerning my career in the field of Human Resources.

Since I had particularly enjoyed my internship, I was disappointed to learn that there were no entry level opportunities available in Human Resources at the time of graduation from Michigan last year. Consequently, I took a position as Human Resources Administrator with Warren Manufacturing Company here in Pittsburgh. My enclosed resume provides further details regarding this position.

Mr. Johnson, I would very much like to return to the Chicago area since my family, and many of my most closest friends, reside in the Greater Chicago Area. I am writing, therefore, to inquire if there are any entry level openings on your staff for which I might be considered. Down deep, I still have a strong interest in working for AHP.

In the event that there are no appropriate openings available at this time, I was wondering if you or any of your staff members could be of assistance to me in my effort to return to Chicago. Perhaps you are aware of others who are looking for someone with my credentials, or there are persons with whom I should be talking, who could be of assistance in my job search. Any general suggestion you might have in this regard would be greatly appreciated.

I will plan to call you sometime in the next few days and would hope that you might have a few moments to spend with me by phone. I really enjoyed our brief relationship, and would value any advice and/or counsel you might be able to provide on this topic.

Thank you very much for your help, and I look forward to speaking with you shortly.

Sincerely,

Lynn Nemser

Lynn E. Nemser

Enclosure

125 Welling Lane
College Park, MD 12996

October 30, 1995

Mr. Richard B. Marsden
Senior Vice President
Human Resources Department
The T. J. Loften Company, Inc.
400 East Carolina Blvd., NE
Washington, DC 12345

Dear Mr. Marsden:

As Chapter President of the Human Resources Management Association for the Greater Washington Metro Area, you are likely to be aware of senior level human resources openings from time to time. I am therefore contacting you to see if you might have some suggestions concerning my job search.

I am currently Vice President of Human Resources for Carson Electronics, a $1.2 billion, 7,000 employee manufacturer of radar components. In my position, I report to the President of Carson and have world-wide responsibility for direction of the Company's Human Resources function. Details of my qualifications are shown on the enclosed resume.

My decision to leave Carson is highly confidential, and I am therefore being particularly discreet with regard to my job search efforts.

I am seeking a senior level Human Resources position with a large manufacturing company, where I will be a member of the senior management team and have broad strategic responsibilities for contributing to the overall direction of the business. My compensation requirements are in the $150,000+ range.

I will plan to touch base with you shortly to determine if you are aware of any openings at this level that would be worth my pursuing. Should you not be aware of any appropriate openings, I would sincerely appreciate any thoughts you might have concerning either my resume or my job hunting strategy. Additionally, perhaps you may be aware of other individuals, with whom I should be in contact, who may be aware of appropriate openings at this level. In any event, I would welcome any ideas and/or assistance you might be able to provide to me.

Thank you very much for your willingness to help, and I look forward to speaking with you personally.

Sincerely,

Fulton J. Royale

Fulton J. Royale

FJR/gs

Enclosure

KERWIN R. MELLON

145 East 42nd Street
New York, NY 12346

Home: (212) 557-1938
Office: (212) 357-9127

June 22, 1996

Ms. Martha R. Rafesnyder
Director of Corporate Planning
Royal Chemical, Ltd.
200 Park Avenue
New York, NY 12948

Dear Ms. Rafesnyder:

I have just completed an MBA at Columbia University in Financial Planning. Your name was given to me by David Mathers, Vice President of Operations, who suggested I contact you. Mr. Mathers and my father, Arthur Mellon, are close personal friends and graduated from Oxford University together.

As my resume will show, I am an honors graduate and hold an undergraduate degree in Mechanical Engineering. My credentials include nearly a year's worth of experience as a Financial Analyst in the Corporate Planning Department of NRG International, a $700 million German-owned chemical manufacturing company. During this time, I was instrumental in assisting NRG in the evaluation of several potential acquisition candidates here in the U.S. I left NRG to complete my final year of graduate study at Columbia.

Mr. Mathers indicated that he thought you might be looking for someone with my credentials for your Corporate Planning Department. If not, however, he felt that you might be willing to provide me with some suggestions and ideas concerning my job search. In particular, he seemed to feel that you might have some ideas about key persons with whom I should be in contact in the chemical industry.

Since I live here in New York, it would be quite easy for me to come to your office for a meeting at a time that is convenient to you. I would certainly welcome the opportunity for such a meeting and would greatly appreciate your general advice and counsel concerning my job search. Hopefully, you will have some time in your busy schedule to meet with me.

Recognizing that you may be difficult to reach, I will plan to contact your secretary in an effort to arrange a convenient time for us to get together. I am totally flexible and would be pleased to meet either during or outside of normal business hours.

Thank you for your assistance, and I look forward to the possibility of meeting with you personally.

Sincerely,

Kerwin R. Mellon

Kerwin R. Mellon

Enclosure

CYNTHIA P. DETWEILER

106 North Collins Ave.
Garden City, CA 12779

Home: (315) 447-9191
Office: (315) 665-2348

January 2, 1997

Dr. Joseph T. Warring
Professor
Business Economics Department
Stamford University
600 Las Verdes Blvd.
Palo Alto, CA 13274

Dear Dr. Warring:

I was speaking to John Tiplon of General Dynamics the other day, and he strongly encouraged me to contact you. I understand that you have done extensive consulting for General Dynamics in the strategic planning area and that you have a number of senior level contacts with the corporate planning functions of a number of the larger U.S. companies. Consequently, John seemed to feel that you might willing to be of some assistance to me with regard to my current job search.

Dr. Warring, I hold an MBA from Harvard University in Finance and have spent the last 25 years in the corporate planning and development field. Currently, I am Senior Vice President - Corporate Planning with McDonald Douglas Corporation, here in Los Angeles.

As the result of some recent changes in senior corporate management, I have elected to confidentially explore a career change. My goal is to find a position as the senior corporate planning officer with a major, multi-billion dollar, high technology company. Compensation requirements would be in the $200,000 range.

John suggested I contact you, thinking that perhaps you could help me to make some key contacts in the industry. I am looking to identify senior level persons, working either in or with the corporate business development function, through whom I might network in identifying an executive level position in my field. In particular, I would like to identify individuals who are professionally very active outside their own organizations and who seem to have a number of professional contacts in the business development field. This could include corporate people, business brokers, capital venture people, key bankers, consultants, and the like.

I have enclosed a copy of my resume for your review and reference.

I will plan to call you early next week, and would greatly appreciate any thoughts that you might have on this subject.

Thank you for your help in this matter, and I look forward to speaking with you personally.

Sincerely,

Cynthia P. Detweiler

Cynthia P. Detweiler

Enclosure

SUE ELLEN ROMANOWSKI

205 Pine Cone Lane   Home: (315) 887-2174
Clayville, NY 13724   Office:(315) 339-2176

August 22, 1996

Mr. Warren L. Harrington
Regional Director
Environmental Protection Agency
300 Erie Avenue
Albany, NY 13295

Dear Mr. Harrington:

I am a recent graduate of R.P.I. with an M.S. degree in Environmental
Engineering. Although an excellent student, in view of the current economic
conditions, I have been experiencing some difficulty in finding meaningful
employment in my field.

In a recent conversation with Senator D'Amato, he suggested I contact you
for some assistance. Senator D'Amato and my father, John Symington, were
close personal friends and worked for many years on various political
committees for the Democratic Party. Specifically, the Senator seemed to
feel that you might be willing to help me identify expanding environmental
consulting firms who may be looking for someone with my credentials.

If your schedule would permit, I would very much like to come to Albany to
discuss this matter with you directly. Perhaps you might also be kind
enough to help me to identify key contacts within the field. I would be
most grateful for any advice and assistance that you might provide
regarding this matter.

I will plan to contact you in a few days to determine if your schedule
would allow us to meet. Thank you for your help, and I look forward to the
possibility of meeting with you personally.

Sincerely,

Sue Ellen Romanowski

Sue Ellen Romanowski

Enclosure

OMAR G. RAMOS
132 Willis Lane
Whitesboro, NY 13492

August 22, 1996

Ms. Barbara T. Cooper
Executive Director
National Association of Public Affairs
200 New Hampshire Avenue, NW
Washington, DC 12968

Dear Barbara:

Greetings from upstate New York! It hardly seems two years ago that we worked so hard together on the national meeting in Atlanta. At least our hard work paid off, and the meeting was a major success. I don't envy you the task of having to do that each and every year. It must be exhausting.

Barbara, I am writing to ask your assistance with my job search. I have decided that I would like to leave the Utica area in favor of warmer climes, and would like to center my search on the southeastern U.S. Both Atlanta and Miami would be of particular interest, however, I am quite flexible in this regard.

As you know, I have been Director of Public Affairs for Carrier Corporation for the last 3 years, and have over 20 years of experience in the field. I have enclosed a complete copy of my resume for your reference. I might mention, that Carrier is totally unaware of my decision, so I would appreciate your handling this inquiry with appropriate sensitivity, which I know you will do.

In your capacity as Executive Director, I know you are contacted from time to time by companies who are looking for senior executives in the Public Affairs field. I would appreciate your keeping me in mind for any such inquiries.

Beyond this, however, I would like to discuss my situation with you and seek your advice regarding the best way to conduct my job search. Any thoughts and ideas you might have on this subject would be greatly appreciated. It has been quite some time since I was last in the job market.

I will plan to call you sometime next week, and hopefully will be able to catch up with you. (I recall what a busy schedule you have.) In the meantime, perhaps you will have an opportunity to review my resume.

I look forward to our conversation, Barbara, and very much appreciate your assistance in this matter. Thank you.

Sincerely,

Omar G. Ramos

Enclosure

BARBARA O. SCHWARTZ
201 Eastwood Avenue
Utica, NY 13501

April 1, 1996

Mr. William T. Sloan
Vice President & General Counsel
Shell Oil Company
200 Royale Oaks Plaza
Houston, TX 13248

Dear Mr. Sloan:

Bill Johnson, one of my colleagues at the Sun Company, suggested that I contact you. I understand that Bill and you began your careers together at DuPont and worked together for nearly 12 years. He speaks very highly of you.

Mr. Sloan, I am a corporate attorney and have worked in the Law Division of the Sun Company for 2 years since my graduation from Harvard Law School in 1994. My area of concentration has been Human Resources law, although I have also been exposed to both patent and antitrust law as well.

I have enclosed a copy of my resume for your reference.

My husband, Stuart, and I have arrived at a mutual decision to relocate to the Houston area. Stuart has been offered the position of General Manager of DuPont's petrochemicals operation, and I have agreed to attempt to find a suitable position that will provide me with the opportunity for future growth and professional development.

Although you may not be aware of any openings for someone with my credentials, Bill seemed to feel that you might be willing to arrange for some personal introductions to some of your professional colleagues with other corporations in the Houston area. As you know, it will be important for me to do extensive networking throughout the local legal community, if I am going to be successful in locating a suitable career opportunity. Anything that you could do to help me in this regard will be very much appreciated.

I will be in Houston the week beginning April 22nd to do some househunting, and was wondering whether your schedule might allow us to get together for either lunch or dinner. I would greatly appreciate your insights concerning the Houston legal community as well as any general suggestions you might have concerning my job search. I will give you a call to see if we can coordinate a convenient time to meet.

Bill sends his best, and wants to know when the two of you are going to vacation in Aruba again. He says he's ready whenever you are.

Thank you for your help, and I look forward to meeting with you while in Houston.

Sincerely,

Barbara O. Schwartz

Barbara O. Schwartz

Enclosure

FRANK B. O'SULLIVAN
305 Sharon Circle, Woodland Hills, Columbus, OH 13958

November 16, 1997

Ms. Marilyn T. Kemp
Senior Partner
Kemp, Sheel, Boussard & Pope
Attorneys at Law
200 Wilton Towers
1800 East Michigan Ave.
Chicago, IL 13958

Dear Marilyn:

I really appreciated the help you gave us last year on the Coated Films Antitrust Case. The defense strategy was magnificent and the victory was sweet indeed. Obviously, we've come to have a high regard for you and your colleagues.

Marilyn, I am writing to you with regard to a personal and highly confidential matter. As a result of some recent changes here at Westlake Corporation, I have decided to quietly leave my position as General Counsel and seek a similar position with a larger company, preferably in manufacturing. I am therefore enclosing a copy of my resume for your reference.

Knowing of your excellent reputation in the field of antitrust law and some of the key national cases your firm has handled for several major U.S. companies, I thought I would quietly contact you to see if you would be willing to be of some assistance relative to my job search. Specifically, I would appreciate the opportunity to meet with you to discuss this matter personally.

Marilyn, I know that you are likely unaware of a specific opening at this time, but I would value your general observations and recommendations concerning my job search strategy, and would appreciate the opportunity to discuss this topic with you on a broader basis. I would personally find such conversation very beneficial. Perhaps we could meet over either lunch or dinner.

I will plan to call your office on Friday of this week to see when you might be available to meet. I look forward to seeing you again, and will very much appreciate your assistance on this subject.

Thank you.

Very truly yours,

Frank

Frank B. O'Sullivan

FBO/sp

Enclosure

MARY ANNE DAVIS
205 Concord Road
Framingham, MA 12847

March 23, 1994

Mr. Corbin A. O'Neil
Manager of MIS Operations
James River Corporation
100 East Gaylord Street
Holyoke, MA 12397

Dear Corbin:

I am a close personal friend of Kate Dobbs, who, I understand, is a colleague of yours at James River. Kate told me to contact you, feeling that you might be willing to help me with a career change that I am considering. I would be very appreciative of your assistance.

As my enclosed resume shows, I am a 1992 graduate of Boston College with a B.S. degree in Computer Science and a minor in Accounting. For the past 2 years, I have been employed as a Programmer/Analyst for HRD Software, a software development firm specializing in the development of computer software with applications in the human resources field. My full resume is enclosed for your reference.

I understand from Kate, that James River has recently undertaken the purchase and installation of a large, broad-based human resources/payroll system. In view of my dual degree and extensive experience with human resources systems, perhaps I may be of some value to you.

Even if you do not have a current opening which is appropriate, I would still like to have the opportunity to meet with you. Perhaps, in exchange for some tips I might be able to pass along on the HR Systems package you bought, you might be willing to provide me with some valuable suggestions and ideas regarding my job search. This could prove to be a mutually beneficial meeting.

I will plan to call you this Friday to see if we might be able to get together. Right now, the weeks beginning April 5th and April 12th would be convenient for me. I am quite flexible, however, and would be pleased to adjust my schedule to accommodate you needs.

Thank you for your assistance, and I look forward to the opportunity of meeting with you personally.

Sincerely,

Mary Anne Davis

Mary Anne Davis

Enclosure

135 West Point Road
Lansdale, PA 19775

July 23, 1995

Ms. Joanne B. Tartan
President
Tartan & Deplinger Associates
1815 JFK Blvd.
Philadelphia, PA 19284

Dear Joanne:

How is the Smith Klein project coming along? I had heard through the grapevine that your firm had landed the multi-million dollar installation and start-up project for SKB's new general ledger system. Congratulations, that's quite a feather in your cap! It just goes to show that, in the long run high quality work and talented people "can" win.

Joanne, I am writing to see if you might be willing to help me with a personal matter. I have arrived at the conclusion that, if I want to experience long-term career growth, I am going to need to leave my position as MIS Development Manager at Wilson Food Corporation. Although the company has been good to me, capital is tight and the company is beginning to cut several corners -- many in the MIS capital projects area. Additionally, future growth prospects for the company look discouraging over the next few years, as the company loses several of its key patent positions to competition.

I know as a consultant in the MIS field, you are well-known and have a number of key contacts. I felt, perhaps, you might be willing to spend a few minutes with me to review my resume and help me with formulation of my job search strategy. Your insights concerning current industry trends and potential opportunity areas could be very beneficial to me at this point in the job hunting process. I would be most appreciative if you could share some of your observations and ideas with me.

How does your calendar look for the week beginning August 8th? Would it be possible for you to join me for a long lunch to discuss this matter?

I will call you in the next day or two to see if we can arrange a convenient time to meet. As always, Joanne, I look forward to meeting with you.

Thank you for your willingness to assist me in this matter.

Sincerely,

Scott M. Murray

Scott M. Murray

SMM/bw

Enclosure

LAWRENCE C. BRADY

600 Manning Blvd.   Home: (218) 377-0921
Miami, FL 16638   Office: (218) 447-9127

                                                     May 26, 1996

Mr. Wilson F. Morse
Regional Sales Manager
Yellow Freight Systems
200 Industry Avenue, SW
Albany, GA 15779

Dear Mr. Morse:

As Regional Sales Manager with Yellow Freight Systems, I am sure you are aware, from time to time, of openings in Distribution Management with some of your customers. Perhaps, one of your customers may be in the market for a young, ambitious Shipping Supervisor with strong potential for growth to senior level management. If so, I may well be an excellent match for their requirements.

As the enclosed resume shows, I hold a B.A. degree in Logistics from the University of Tennessee, and have slightly over 2 years experience as a Shipping Supervisor for Carnation Company at their regional warehouse here in Miami. In fact, we have been a major customer of yours and frequently use Yellow Freight for a lot of our overnight hauls throughout the southeastern United States.

The next time you are in the Miami area, I would appreciate the opportunity to meet with you. As a result of your extensive contacts and knowledge of the distribution industry, it would likely be very beneficial to talk with you about my career. I would sincerely appreciate any general thoughts and/or ideas that you feel could be helpful to my career search.

I will call your office shortly, to see if your secretary could arrange such a meeting for me. This is, of course, highly confidential, since Carnation Company is totally unaware of my decision.

I look forward to the prospects of meeting with you, Mr. Morse, and would sincerely appreciate your willingness to share ideas and suggestions with me on this topic. Thank you very much.

                                                     Sincerely,

                                                     Lawrence Brady

                                                     Lawrence C. Brady

Enclosure

SIDNEY S. SMALL

125 Oneida Way   Home: (712) 336-9128
New Hartford, NY 12579   Office: (712) 227-1894

September 14, 1994

Ms. Carolyn W. Dawson
Director of Procurement
Millington Corporation
600 Commerce Street
Albany, NY 18375

Dear Carolyn:

It was nice seeing you again at the National Association of Purchasing Agents meeting in Albany this past Spring. Time has really flown, and it hardly seems 6 months ago that Gary, you and I were having dinner together at McCarthy's. That's something we need to do more than just once a year. I have always thoroughly enjoyed our time together.

Unfortunately, Carolyn, I find myself needing to face a more serious matter. Utica Steel Corporation has just announced its decision to shut down its furnace operations in Whitehall, which means that as of November 1st I will be "on the street". I only wish they had given us a little more warning of this. With two kids currently in college, things are going to be a bit tight.

I know how active you have been over the years in NAPA, and have always admired your ability to get things done through your many personal contacts in the Association. Right now, I wish I were as well "networked" as you. It would certainly come in handy.

If your schedule would permit, I like to meet you for lunch sometime in the next week or so. (I'm buying!) I would really appreciate your thoughts and ideas concerning my job search strategy. It has been quite some time since I have had to look for a job, and I'm afraid that my skills are more than just a bit rusty.

As a prelude to our meeting, I am enclosing a "draft" copy of my resume and would appreciate if you could look it over. In addition, I would like to ask you to give some thought to key contacts who are well-connected in the Purchasing field. I need to begin to prepare a list of primary contacts, through whom I can network to identify an appropriate career opportunity.

I hate to dump all of this on you, but I'm really not sure where to turn at the moment. You've always been a great friend, and I know that I can count on you to help me. If you ever need help, I'm sure you already know that I will be there to lend a hand. Hopefully, you'll never need to face this one. At age 58, it's not going to be easy!

Carolyn, I'll call you later this week, and we can work out the details of where and when to meet. Thanks for your help.

Best regards,

Sid

Sidney S. Small

Enclosure

CONSTANCE A. PARKER

123 Greenlawn Drive
Norwalk, CT 12668

Home: (318) 227-4858
Office:(212) 667-3749

February 26, 1994

Mr. Giles Richard
Quality Control Manager
Barlow Chemical Company
125 River Street
Bridgeport, CT 12674

Dear Giles:

I have recently made a decision to leave Gilbert Laboratories, where I have been a Quality Engineer for the past 2 years. When discussing this matter with Gary Peterson the other day, he suggested that I contact you. Gary felt you might be in a positon to provide me with some good advice.

Giles, clearly I am not expecting you will be aware of a job opportunity. Instead, I was hopeful that you might spend a few minutes with me on the phone to share any ideas you might have concerning my job search. In particular, I was hoping that you might suggest some key contacts in the quality field with whom I should be in touch as part of my job search.

Generally, the kinds of people that could prove most beneficial to know, are those who are well-connected and appear to know a number of other professionals and managers in the quality field. This might include such persons as professionals & managers working directly in the quality field, vendors who sell products and services to the quality field, consultants, key professors, etc. I would greatly appreciate if you could help me to identify such persons.

In anticipation of our conversation, I have enclosed a copy of my resume for your review and reference. I would also welcome any suggestions you might have on ways to improve the effectiveness of this document.

Anything that you could do to help me with my job search effort will be greatly appreciated. Thank you very much for your help, and I look forward to talking with you.

Sincerely,

Constance A. Parker

Enclosure

ROBERT D. BUZINSKI
206 Whitehall Road
Oneida, NY 13746

August 22, 1995

Ms. Linda R. Bessimer
Senior Quality Consultant
The Quality Equation, Inc.
207 Park Avenue, North
Wilton, CT 14680

Dear Linda:

I am writing at the suggestion of John Eden, Vice President of Quality at Ford Electronics Company, who thought perhaps you might be of assistance to me. John and I have known one another for several years, and are close personal friends.

During lunch with John yesterday, he mentioned that you had contacted him to let him know that General Electric was looking for a Director of Total Quality for their Power Products Division in Syracuse. I understand that you had been contacted by a search firm, but John couldn't recall which one.

Based upon what John has told me about this position, it would appear that I may well be a very good match for their requirements. I have both an undergraduate degree in engineering and a graduate degree in Statistics. I have spent the last 18 years in the quality field, the last 4 of which have been as Manager of Total Quality for IBM's Industrial Controls Division. I have enclosed a copy of my resume for your reference.

Since I would be interested in pursuing this position, I will plan to give you a call shortly. In the meantime, I would appreciate if you could confidentially pass along a copy of my resume to the search firm that contacted you.

Additionally, Linda, I would appreciate the opportunity to talk with you more broadly about my job search. Perhaps you may have ideas on key persons with whom I should be in contact during the course of my search. I would certainly welcome an suggestions you may have on this matter.

Thank you for passing my resume along, and I look forward to speaking with you shortly.

Sincerely,

Bob Buzinski

Robert D. Buzinski

Enclosure

WILMA E. DAVIDSON

17 Southwood Drive, Wilbraham, MA 17239

June 12, 1996

Mr. William C. Hartman
Regional Sales Manager
WITCO Chemical Company
201 Mayflower Avenue
Boston, MA 16932

Dear Bill:

I am writing to you on a confidential basis to seek your help on a personal matter. As you know, we have had some changes here at General Foam, and I am now reporting to Bill Prescott, Vice President. I do not view this as a positive move and, as a result, I have elected to make a career change.

Although you are already somewhat familiar with my credentials, I have enclosed a copy of my resume to fill in the gaps. Highlights include a B.S. degree in Chemical Engineering and nearly 4 years experience in chemicals procurement. All of this has been with General Foam.

At this point in my career, I am looking for a junior level management position in the procurement department of a major corporation, where there is the opportunity for long-term career growth. Of course, I would want to remain in the chemical process industry. Compensation requirements are in the low to mid $60,000 range, dependent upon opportunity and location.

With your large number of contacts in the procurement field in the chemical process related industries, I felt that perhaps you might be aware of someone looking for a candidate with my credentials. Additionally, I would appreciate of you could share with me the names of some key contacts in the industry, with whom it would be a good idea to touch base during the course of my job search.

When you are in the Springfield area next Wednesday, I wonder if you might have some time to spend with me on this topic. Perhaps we might have lunch or dinner together. I would also welcome your overall general advice and counsel on my job search strategy.

I recognize the potential sensitivity of this, so I want to assure you of my utmost confidentiality regarding any help which you provide. Likewise, as I'm sure you can appreciate, my decision to make a career move at this time is also a highly confidential and sensitive matter.

Bill, I will call you to see if we can work something out to meet. Thank you for helping me with this matter.

Sincerely,

Wilma Davidson

Wilma E. Davidson

Enclosure

JACK B. PASCAL
120 Country Club Lane
Buffalo, NY 13286

October 21, 1997

Mr. Willis T. Broderick
President
Dow Chemical Company
1 Dow Plaza
Midland, MI 13249

Dear Will:

I recently heard from Melody that Chris and you went bone fishing near Captiva and had a great time. This puts me in mind of our great adventure sailfishing 2 years ago in Aruba. I can't recall when I've had more fun. You always had a soft touch when it comes to going game fishing. Perhaps I could tempt you away from your work again this year to give it another try. What do you think?

Speaking of "soft touch", I'm afraid I'm going to need your help. It seems that Chemco Products is going to be sold to DuPont, and I'm told that my position as Vice President of Procurement is to be eliminated. So, I thought I had better launch my job search sooner rather than later.

I am enclosing an advance copy of my resume, Will, and would like to arrange to meet with you as soon as your hectic schedule will permit. I would really appreciate your advice and counsel on my job search.

I will give Sarah a call this Friday to see when we could get together. Could you please alert her to my need to meet with you?

As always, I am indebted to your generosity and look forward to our meeting. Please say "hello" to Melody for me, and tell her I "send my love".

Warmest regards,

Jack

Jack B. Pascal

JBP/sd

Enclosure

SANDRA B. JACKSON
122 Elm Tree Road
Fort Wayne, IN 42958
(413) 475-9684

July 16, 1997

Mr. Wilbur R. Hawthorne
Director of Marketing
National Electronics, Inc.
835 Powell Blvd.
Indianapolis, IN 43576

Dear Will:

You may recall that we met briefly last summer at Sam Morrow's 4th of July picnic. During a recent conversation with Sam, he suggested that I contact you and reminded me of our meeting.

Will, unfortunately, my company, Nastar Electronics, has just been sold to Wilshire Corporation and my services as National Sales Manager are no longer required. Wilshire is simply folding the Nastar product line into their existing sales organization which, of course, is headed by their own Director of Sales & Marketing. Friday will be my last day.

I will be in the Indianapolis area the week beginning the 28th and would like to meet you for lunch, should your schedule allow. I was hopeful that you might be able to share some thoughts and general advice concerning my job search. Sam says that you are quite knowledgeable of the electronics communications market and might have some general suggestions about possible job hunting strategies. I would sincerely welcome any thoughts you might have on this subject.

By way of preliminary introduction to this topic, I have enclosed a copy of my resume for your review.

I hope your schedule will allow us to get together and that you will be able to join me. I will give you a call early next week to see what your schedule looks like, and we can go from there.

Thanks for your help, and I look forward to having lunch with you.

Sincerely,

Sandy Jackson

Sandra B. Jackson

SBJ/dap

Enclosure

CHRISTOPHER R. BANNISTER

116 Sandy Hook Road, Ocean Park, CA 12847

May 16, 1996

Ms. Katherine B. Foster
Director of Corporate Accounting
The Melloncamp Corporation
816 Tower Hill Circle
San Francisco, CA 12385

Dear Kathy:

The other day in a conversation with Linda Banks, your name came up. I was telling Linda about my recent decision to leave my current position as General Ledger Accountant with Telstar Corporation to seek a position offering greater growth potential, when Linda suggested that I give you a call. I understand the two of you were sorority sisters at Arizona State together and still stay in close touch.

Kathy, I am certainly not expecting that you will be aware of a job for me. Instead, my interest in talking with you is much broader than that. What I was hoping was that you might have a few minutes to spend with me to review my resume and provide me with some general advice regarding my current job search. I would very much value your counsel.

I will plan to call you shortly to see when might be a convenient time for us to get together. I sincerely appreciate your assistance with my job search and look forward to our discussion.

By the way, Linda says to say "hello" and to tell you that she is planning to go to the reunion at Arizona in June. She will plan to give you a call to see if the two of you can go together.

Thanks again for your help, and I look forward to the possibility of meeting with you.

Sincerely

Christopher R. Bannister

Enclosure

CONSTANCE B. REEDER

123 Shady Hollow Road
College Park, MD 13683

Home: (213) 779-3254
Office: (213) 775-3246

October 3, 1995

Mr. Wilson L. Goodman
President
The Goodman Group, Inc.
1625 Maryland Avenue, NE
Washington, DC 13232

Dear Wilson:

Bud Smith and I were talking the other day, and he mentioned that you own and operate a very successful graphics arts firm that does a lot of contract work for the J. Walter Thompson Agency in consumer goods advertising. As a result, Bud seemed to feel that you might be in a position to assist me, and suggested that I contact you.

Wilson, until Friday of last week, I was the Creative Director for the VanHeuster Advertising Agency here in College Park. Unfortunately, due to the sudden and unexpected death of Bill VanHeuster, the owner, his widow has elected to close the business. This leaves me in the position of seeking employment.

Rather than bore you with a lot of detail in this letter, I have decided to enclose a copy of my resume for your reference. In short, I have a Masters degree in Graphic Arts and over 10 years experience on the creative side of a small family-owned consumer products advertising firm.

Bud seemed to feel that, as a result of your position and contacts in the advertising field, you might be in a position to help me with my job search. Although you may well not be aware of a specific opening, I would very much value spending an hour or so with you to get your overview of the advertising industry and some general suggestions concerning my job search strategy. I sincerely hope you will be able to meet with me.

Wilson, I will plan to give you a call later this week to see if we can arrange a mutually agreeable time to meet.

Thank you for your willingness to be of help.

Very truly yours,

Constance B. Reeder

Enclosure

JAMES D. SHIELDS
325 Reservoir Road
Media, PA 19348
(215) 875-2847

March 22, 1996

Mr. Dennis R. Weaver
Senior Vice President
Rohm & Haas Company
600 East Walnut Street
Philadelphia, PA 19385

Dear Dennis:

I am a neighbor of Bill Davis, and have known Bill for over 15 years. I understand from Bill that the two of you grew up together in the Germantown area and went on to Princeton University together. Bill suggested that I contact you, feeling that perhaps you could be of help to me.

As you are likely aware, DuPont is preparing for another sizeable downsizing and will be offering a voluntary separation package to all of its engineering staff shortly. Since I have been with the company for over 14 years I expect to receive a fairly attractive financial package as part of this offering. I am giving serious consideration to accepting this offer and seeking career opportunities elsewhere.

Dennis, I would very much appreciate the opportunity to meet with you at your convenience to get a better feel for the market. Bill tells me that you have been very active with the American Institute of Chemical Engineers over the years and have a number of key contacts in the chemical industry. Additionally, in your capacity as the head of Rohm & Haas' Engineering & Technology Group, Bill seemed to feel you probably have a fairly good overview of conditions and trends in the chemical industry.

Although I don't expect that you will be aware of specific jobs, I would greatly value your general advice and counsel concerning my job hunting strategy as well any relevant market information that you could provide which might impact my decision to either stay or leave the DuPont Company.

As a prelude to our meeting, I have taken the liberty of enclosing a copy of my resume for your reference. I will plan to call your office this Tuesday to see when it might be convenient for you to meet with me. I sincerely hope that your schedule will permit us to get together in the near future.

Thank you for your help, and I look forward to talking with you on Tuesday.

Sincerely,

James D. Shields

James D. Shields

Enclosure

CYNTHIA W. CUMMINGS
226 Sunnyway Lane
Princeton, NJ 14562
(609) 474-0968

June 3, 1996

Mr. William B. Carver
Vice President Human Resources
Quaker Computer Company
325 Technology Drive
Cherry Hill, NJ 13485

Dear Bill:

You are no doubt aware of the current turmoil at Wilson Computer Technology, and the substantial losses that the company has experienced over the last two years. The continuing uncertainty of this situation has caused me to decide to seek employment opportunities elsewhere.

I have long known Dick Thomas through the Employment Management Association and our time together on the Board and various committees. In recent conversation with Dick, he suggested that I contact you, feeling that perhaps you could be of some help to me in my job search.

Briefly, I have an MBA from Rutgers University and 8 years of Human Resources experience in the electronics industry. For the last 5 years, I have been Director of Employment for Wilson Computer Technology. A copy of my resume is enclosed for your reference.

Although you are not likely to be aware of specific job opportunities, Bill, it would be helpful if I could meet with you for an hour or so concerning my job search. I would appreciate the opportunity to discuss my job hunting strategy with you and get the benefit of your counsel concerning my approach. I would also appreciate any ideas and suggestions you might have concerning key persons within the industry with whom I should be in contact for employment networking purposes.

I will plan to contact your secretary early next week to see if your schedule will allow us to get together. I would really appreciate the opportunity to meet with you and hope that you can find some time to share some of your thoughts and ideas with me.

Thank you, and I look forward to the possibility of meeting with you in the near future.

Sincerely,

Cynthia B. Cummings

Enclosure

DANIEL R. MURPHY
133 Wild Creek Road
Westbrook, ME 13285
(316) 447-4958

June 15, 1996

Ms. Phylis A. Cheyney
Director of Marketing
L.L. Bean, Inc.
325 Bass Road
Portland, ME 13259

Dear Phylis:

Last evening, following our weekly tennis match, I mentioned to Dave Curry that I was considering leaving my position as National Sales Manager for Bass Shoes here in Portland. Dave mentioned that he knew you quite well and strongly suggested that I give you a call. He felt, as a result of your position at L.L. Bean, you might have some ideas or suggestions for me about my job hunting campaign.

Phylis, if it wouldn't be too much of an imposition, I would really appreciate the opportunity to meet with you. Perhaps we could get together over lunch in the next week or so. I would very much value hearing your views on the state of the retail industry and trends that might have some bearing on my employment decision. I would also appreciate your thoughts on key persons who are knowledgeable of the industry and with whom I should be in contact for networking purposes as I begin my job search.

Since you will need to know more about my background and overall qualifications, I have enclosed a copy of my resume for your review and reference. Your review and suggestions concerning ways in which this resume might be improved would also be very additive to my employment campaign.

I would very much appreciate the opportunity to meet with you, and hope that your schedule will allow us to get together shortly. I will call you on Thursday to check your schedule and see if we can arrange a convenient time to meet.

Phylis, thank you for helping me with this matter, and I look forward to meeting you.

Sincerely,

Daniel R. Murphy

Enclosure

6

The Resume Letter

The resume letter is a cross between a cover letter and a resume. First, it is a cover letter in that it is used to transmit your credentials to the employer. Secondly, it is a replacement for the resume and is designed to provide a brief summary of your employment qualifications. It is thus used to both transmit and sell your credentials to the prospective employer.

The popularity and use of the resume letter have grown considerably over the last few years, and more and more of these letters are showing up in corporate and search firm mailboxes. The proliferation of these documents, however, is not necessarily a testimonial to their effectiveness as a job-hunting technique. There appears to be no concrete evidence that they are any more effective than the conventional cover letter and resume combination.

ADVANTAGES OF RESUME LETTER

Proponents of the resume letter will argue that there are certain advantages realized by the job seeker in use of the resume letter when contrasted with use of the conventional cover letter and resume. The advantages typically cited by these individuals are as follows:

1. A one-page letter format is far more likely to be read than a two or three-page letter and resume format.
2. If well-written, the resume letter provides just enough information to stimulate curiosity and interest, but not too much information to allow the candidate to be "screened out" by the employer.
3. By providing only a limited amount of information, employers will need to call the candidate to get more. This provides candidates with an op-

portunity to "sell themselves"—an opportunity not normally afforded to those sending a "complete" resume.

4. Because of the number of multipage, unsolicited resumes received by most managers and employment professionals, these individuals will "appreciate" the one-page resume letter.

5. Where cost is a factor, the use of a one-page resume letter, versus a multipage cover letter and resume packet, can be considerably cheaper. Use of the one-page approach allows the job hunter to "survey" a much larger employer audience for the same cost as a much smaller multipage mailing.

On the surface these arguments sound good. Certainly, there seems to be ample logic present to support these contentions. To put things into better perspective, however, one needs to consider the disadvantages of the resume letter, before blindly accepting it as a job search panacea and the centerfold of one's job-hunting campaign.

DISADVANTAGES OF RESUME LETTER

The truth of the matter is that most employment professionals, in my opinion, view the resume letter with a certain amount of disdain. Major disadvantages cited by this group include the following:

1. Resume letters usually contain insufficient information to determine if the candidate is qualified for a given opening.

2. Lack of detailed information does not allow the employer to determine the "degree" of qualification for a given position.

3. Insufficient information does not allow a proper comparison with other qualified candidates, placing the user of the resume letter at considerable competitive disadvantage.

4. Busy employment and line managers are loathe to pick up the telephone and call a candidate to simply determine whether he or she has the basic qualifications for an opening. Most will call *only* as a last resort, when there are no other qualified candidates identified. They do not wish to waste their time talking with candidates who are potentially "unqualified" for an open position.

5. Users of resume letters may sometimes be viewed as "suspicious" or "deceptive" by employers. Why else would they not furnish a complete accounting of their qualifications and experience as provided for in the standard resume format?

6. Some employers may view users of resume letters as lazy—unwilling to commit the necessary time and effort to prepare a proper resume document.

Obviously this is a healthy list of disadvantages, which might well discourage conscientious job seekers from using the resume letter as part of their job-hunting strategy. Time is still out on this method however and, as of yet, there are no good statistics available that either confirm or refute the effectiveness of this job search technique. So one cannot simply write it off as worthless.

In my judgement, the resume letter is likely to be far more effective when mailed directly to functional managers (those who have the openings) rather than to the employment manager or personnel department. These line managers normally receive far fewer resumes and employment letters than does the busy human resources executive. As a result, therefore, I believe there is a far better chance that your letter will be read and that a telephone conversation might ensue.

So, in the final analysis, it might be worth trying the use of the resume letter to conduct a broad-based mail "survey" campaign to functional managers at several hundred companies. Certainly, it will be a lot less expensive to do this than to mail a full resume and letter packet. This will allow you to reach a much larger group of employers at far less cost.

Additionally, I should mention that I believe the use of the resume letter may prove far more effective when serving as the basis for a mass mail campaign to search firms and/or employment agencies. In such case, the financial incentive (the placement fees they collect from client companies) is probably sufficient reward to motivate the search consultant to pick up a telephone and call the prospective candidate. Most live on the phone anyway and are accustomed to speaking with several unqualified candidates on the way to finding those few who will satisfy their client's needs.

COMPONENTS OF EFFECTIVE RESUME LETTERS

If a resume letter is going to succeed, it must be well-designed and well-written. Review of the several sample resume letters that comprise the balance of this chapter will reveal that there are certain key components that increase the effectiveness of these letters as a job-hunting tool. These are as follows:

1. Statement of Interest in Employment
2. Statement of Job Search Objective (Position Sought)
3. Broad Summary of Relevant Qualifications to Include:
    a. Educational Credentials
    b. Job-Related Experience
    c. Important Traits and Characteristics
4. Summary of Important Job-Relevant Accomplishments
5. Salary and Geographical Requirements (Optional)
6. Request for Employer Action

7. Specific Contact Instructions (Optional)

8. Statement of Appreciation for Consideration

Sufficient sample resume letters have hopefully been provided in this chapter to assist you in modeling an effective resume letter of your own. I would suggest that you review them carefully before deciding on the format that will best suit your specific needs.

JORDAN D. MARSHALL

130 Deerview Creek **Grand Rapids, MI 18669**	**Home:** (416) 337-5959 **Office:** (416) 468-1847

August 22, 1995

Mr. Quentin T. Broome
Senior Vice President
Marketing & Sales
NASA Electronics, Inc.
330 Technology Drive
Atlanta, GA 16485

Dear Mr. Broome:

I am a highly successful National Sales Manager with an excellent, documentable record of accomplishment in the sale of electronic components to O.E.M. accounts in the defense industry. Highlights of my background include:

- B.S. and M.S. degrees in Electrical Engineering

- Direct 80 person national and international field salesforce, selling direct and through distributors

- Products include microwave antennae and receiver components for military guidance and tracking systems

Key accomplishments include:

- Revamped field sales organization and market approach, driving sales from $25 million to $126 million in only 4 years

- Successfully introduced 6 new products -- all achieving sales volume which exceeded business plan objectives (2 by more than 50%)

- Reduced cost-of-sales by 18% over 2 year period

I am seeking a senior sales executive position with a high-tech electronics parts manufacturer, where there will be the opportunity to manage both the sales and marketing functions. Position could be at either the corporate or division level. My compensation requirements are a base salary of at least $125,000 plus significant incentive compensation potential based upon contribution.

If my credentials interest you, I can be reached at the numbers shown above on this letterhead. I look forward to hearing from you.

Thank you for your consideration.

Sincerely,

Jordan D. Marshall

Jordan D. Marshall

255 Purdeel Ave.
Mobile, Al 13958

June 6 ,1997

Mr. Lucian J. Codwell
President
Codwell, Johnson & Wilson, Inc.
300 Bay Avenue
Mobile, AL 13947

Dear Mr. Codwell:

I am a talented and energetic Sales Representative with 3 years experience in the sale of paper converting equipment to the paper industry. My accomplishments include:

- Sales Representative of the Year, Southeast Region, 1996

- 3 Years of Significant Sales Volume Increase as Follows:

    1996 = 25% Increase ($100 million to $125 million)

    1995 = 33% Increase ($ 75 million to $100 million)

    1994 = 25% Increase ($ 60 million to $ 75 million)

- Landed Company's Largest Single Account ($12 million)

Products sold include winders, slitters, folders, wrappers, carton machines and sealing equipment. Current territory covers Florida, Georgia and Alabama. Sales are direct and through manufacturer representatives.

I am ready for my first sales management position, and am seeking a position at the district or regional management level with a firm offering the opportunity for advancement into senior sales management positions.

Current compensation includes a base salary of $60,000 plus bonus ($20,000 in 1996).

Please contact me, should any of your clients be looking for someone with my credentials. My home phone is (205) 333-8585.I will be pleased to furnish a complete resume at the appropriate time.

I look forward to hearing from you.

Sincerely,

Patricia L. Gilbert

Patricia L. Gilbert

BARBARA E. EBERLIE

3004 Cove Road
Hampton Beach, NH 16284

Home: (215) 377-2938
Office: (215) 443-1938

January 15, 1997

Mr. Jamie F. Boswell
Vice President Marketing
Mohler Food Corporation
201 Puritan Blvd.
Boston, MA 17458

Dear Mr. Bostwell:

If you are currently looking for a accomplished Brand Manager with strong consumer products background, you may want take a look at my credentials. I have the education, experience and track record that clearly demonstrates my qualifications to play a major role in the successful undertaking of major marketing initiatives.

My qualifications include:

- MBA in Marketing, Harvard University

- 3 Years Marketing Brand Management Experience - Fortune 100 consumer products company

My accomplishments include:

- Led Successful Introduction of Major New Shampoo Line Achieving 15% Market Penetration ($300 Million Sales) in 2 Years

- Successfully Repositioned Failing Detergent Line Increasing Sales by 325% in 3 Year Period

- Generated Highly Creative Advertising Theme for Stagnate Product Line Accounting for Increase in Market Share of 28 points

I have the knowledge, creativity and drive to bring similar accomplishments to Mohler Foods, given the right support and opportunity. In exchange, I am looking for the opportunity to achieve accelerated compensation and career growth commensurate with the level of my contribution to the company.

Should you wish to explore how I might help your organization to get its marketing program in high gear, I would welcome the opportunity to meet with you.

Since my search is confidential, I would appreciate if you would contact me at my home. An answering machine will take your message, and I can be back to you the following business day. Thank you for your consideration.

Sincerely,

Barbara E. Eberlie

Barbara E. Eberlie

HORACE P. THOMPSON

304 South Cliffs Road
Redwood, CA 16233

Home: (415) 875-2938
Office: (415) 227-9128

October 19, 1997

Ms. Beverly C. Wilkes
President
Wilkes, Carson & Smith
10 Tower Drive
San Francisco, CA 15739

Dear Ms. Wilkes:

I am seeking an equity position as a Partner in a small to medium-sized marketing consulting firm. I have strong credentials and can bring the Fortune 100 marketing perspective to an emerging consulting practice.

Consider the following credentials:

- MBA in Marketing, University of Southern California

- 25 Years Marketing Experience as follows:

        5 Years = V.P. Marketing, Clorox Corporation
        3 Years = Director of Marketing, Scott Paper Co.
        5 Years = Sr. Brand Manager, Campbell Soup Co.
        3 Years = Brand Manager, Campbell Soup Co.
        2 Years = Brand Manager, Kraft Foods Co.
        2 Years = Assoc. Brand Manager, Kraft Foods Co.
        3 Years = Sr. Marketing Analyst, Kraft Foods Co.
        2 Years = Market Research Analyst, Kraft Foods Co.

My years of experience are replete with marketing success stories, with major contributions easily documented in all marketing categories from new product introductions, to brand repositioning, through successful national roll-out of numerous product lines.

At this stage in my career, I would like to step back from the corporate political environment and once again focus my energies on the technical side of marketing.

I have considerable experience and numerous contacts that could well benefit a growing consulting firm that is looking to penetrate the major consumer product companies.

If what I have told you is of interest, let me suggest we meet to further explore the strengths that I could bring to your firm. Confidential calls can be placed to my office at the number shown in the above letterhead. I look forward to hearing from you, and thank you for your consideration.

Sincerely,

Horace P. Thompson

Horace P. Thompson

KATHERINE L. NUSSLE
84 Strath Haven Drive
Bryn Mawr, PA 19006

January 20, 1996

Mr. Cleveland R. Parker
Operations Manager
Champion International Corporation
132 Canal Road
New Hope, PA 19337

Dear Mr. Parker:

I am a young, ambitious project engineer looking for an opportunity to break into operations management. Specifically, I am looking for a position as a Shift Supervisor or Department Manager in a papermaking or converting operation, where I can put my technical knowledge and leadership skills to work.

The following is a short synopsis of my credentials:

- B.S. Mechanical Engineering, Bucknell University

- 1 Year as Senior Project Engineer - Papermaking

- 2 Years as Project Engineer - Converting

I have strong interpersonal and leadership skills. These have been clearly demonstrated through my on-campus activities while at Bucknell. Evidence of these skills includes:

- Sorority President, Senior Year
- Sorority Vice President, Junior Year
- Sorority Pledge Master, Sophomore Year
- Captain, Women's' Varsity Swim Team, Senior Year
- President, Amer. Soc. of Mechanical Engineers

I am now ready to make my career transition from technical support to line manufacturing management. With my combination of strong technical and leadership skills, coupled with considerable energy and enthusiasm, I feel my new employer will experience an outstanding return on their investment.

I hope you have heard enough to stimulate your interest, and that I will be hearing from you shortly.

Thank you for your consideration.

Very truly yours,

Katherine L. Nussle
Katherine L. Nussle

KAREN B. ANDERSON

235 Primrose Lane, Albany Georgia 18266

August 25, 1996

Mr. Wilson G. Englender
Vice President of Operations
Georgia Pacific Corporation
100 Peachtree Ave, NE
Atlanta, GA 18246

Dear Mr. Englender:

I am currently employed in Operations Management with one of your key competitors, Procter & Gamble, and have decided to make a career change. I am seeking a senior level operations management position at the division or corporate level, with multi-plant P&L responsibility.

In my current position as General Manager of P&G's Albany Plant, I am responsible for overall management of a 1,500 employee papermaking and converting facility involved in the manufacture of sanitary tissue and household paper products. This mill includes 4 twin-wire Yankee tissues machines and full converting facilities.

Educationally, my qualifications include a B.S. degree in Mechanical Engineering from the University of Wisconsin and an MBA from Duke. I have had considerable management training while with P&G, including several courses related to the development and utilization of "high performance work teams". Additionally, I have been thoroughly schooled in modern manufacturing systems and concepts including SPC-based total quality, MRP, JIT, etc.

My experience at P&G has prepared me well to assume senior level management responsibilities in a major pulp and paper company. During my 15 years with the company, I have advanced through a series of functional assignments including engineering, engineering management, human resources management, distribution management, and operations management. I have held key operations management positions in both papermaking and converting.

Throughout my career, I have continuously maintained the highest possible performance ratings, and my operations have always rated upon the top 10% in operating efficiencies within the Paper Division. During the last 2 years the Albany Plant, for example, has been rated the best overall performing plant site and has received P&G's coveted "Plant of the Year" award.

Mr. Englender, should you have a need for a senior level manufacturing executive with a strong record of achievement in the manufacturer of consumer paper products, I would welcome the opportunity to meet with you. I can be reached during evening hours at my home phone -- (205) 221-9284.

Thank you for your consideration.

Sincerely,

Karen B Anderson

Karen B. Anderson

DAVID V. CONNARD
Apt. 25–B
Lakeview Apartments
126 Glenore Drive
Minneapolis, MN 12368

October 15, 1995

Mr. Oliver D. North
Engineering Manager
3M Corporation
3M Plaza
Minneapolis, MN 12365

Dear Mr. North:

I am a young, hard-working Control Systems Engineer with 2 years plant project engineering experience in the design, installation and start-up of computer control systems on high-speed web handling equipment. My background and experience would appear to be well-suited to your web product manufacturing processes.

Highlights of my qualifications include:

- B.S. Degree, Systems Engineering, Un. of Wisconsin

- 2 Years, Control Systems Engineering,
  Kimberly-Clark Corporation, Neenah Plant

- Engineering Design, Installation and Start-Up of
  $5 million TDC 3000 Control System Project
  (Paper Machine and Converting Equipment)

  Project Included Engineering of Complete
  System --- Computers, Instrumentation and Related
  Control Devices

I am seeking a position at the senior project engineering or supervisory level in the control systems area. My compensation requirements are in the high $40K range.

Should you be in the market for a strong control systems professional or manager, I would welcome the opportunity to meet with you. I can be reached at my office, on a confidential basis, during business hours. My office phone is (414) 372-9485.

Thank you for your consideration, and I look forward to hearing from you.

Sincerely,

David V. Connard

David V. Connard

120 Wildflower Road
Boulder, CO 18273

March 29, 1997

Dr. William B. Martin
Vice President of Engineering
General Dynamics Corporation
200 Commerce & Industry Blvd.
Palo Alto, CA 16559

Dear Dr. Martin:

If you are in search of a senior level engineering executive to manage your company's central engineering department, you may want to give serious consideration to my candidacy.

Highlights of my qualifications include:

- M.S. Electrical Engineering, M.I.T.
  B.S. Mechanical Engineering, M.I.T.

- MBA, Finance, Stanford University

- 25 Years Engineering/ Engineering Management Experience
  As Follows:

  5 Years = V.P. Engineering, Ford Aerospace
  4 Years = Director Engineering, Ford Aerospace
  6 Years = Manager Corp. Engineering, Hughes Aircraft
  4 Years = Dept. Mgr - Mech. Design, Hughes Aircraft
  6 Years = Engr./Sr. Project Engr., Boeing Corporation

In my current position as Vice President of Engineering for Ford Aerospace, I manage a 600 employee central engineering group responsible for all capital project work throughout the company. This includes engineering and start-up of complete manufacturing plants, installation of new manufacturing lines in existing facilities, and major rebuild work. Annual capital budget is in the $1 to $1.5 billion range.

I have established an excellent reputation for the quality and quantity of capital project work completed by my organization, and have a strong reputation as both a demanding and fair leader. Most of the engineering project work performed under my direction has come in at or below budget, and I enjoy an excellent reputation for meeting key project deadlines.

My decision to leave Ford is a confidential one, and the company is totally unaware of my current job search. Current compensation is in the high $100K range.

Should you have an interest in my credentials, I would be pleased to meet with you to explore the contributions that I could make to your engineering efforts. My home phone number is (514) 273-3849.

Thank you.

Sincerely,

Kenneth R. Jamieson

Kenneth R. Jamieson

LYNN S. NEMSER, Ph.D.

805 South Fork Road   Home: (205) 877-3928
Arlington, TX 13948   Office: (205) 722-6846

October 22, 1997

Dr. Keith C. Reinhart
Research Manager
Virology Department
Bristol-Meyers Squibb Company
110 Princeton Pike
Princeton, NJ 08543-4000

Dear Dr. Reinhart:

I am a Research Investigator with over ten years experience in antiviral related research. I am very much aware of the work that your department is doing in this area, and would be interested in exploring opportunities as a member of your research staff.

My credentials include a Ph.D. in Molecular Biology from the University of Pennsylvania, where I spent six years in a post-doctoral program doing basic research related to virology. Since then I have been employed as a research scientist in the Antiviral Department of Merck & Company. Inc., where I have conducted independent research studies to define unique viral targets for antiviral intervention and have collaborated with other research groups in the design and development of novel antiviral agents.

The basic research budget at Merck has recently been cut, and several of my research projects have been adversely affected. Consequently, I am looking for a company that has a strong commitment to its basic research programs and is heavily funding projects in the antiviral area. Bristol-Meyers Squibb Company appears to fit these criteria rather well.

My current annual compensation is $68,000, and I would require an offer in the mid $70K range in order to give serious consideration to making a career move.

Should you have an interest in my credentials, Dr. Reinhart, I would welcome the opportunity to meet with you to explore how I might contribute to your research programs and objectives. I can be reached at my home during the evening or, on a confidential basis, at my office during the day.

Thank you for considering me, and I look forward to hearing from you.

Very truly yours,

Lynn S. Nemser

Lynn S. Nemser

WILLIAM M. MORRIS, Ph.D.

603 West Lear Street
Seattle, WA 12847

Home: (206) 997-2239
Office: (206) 756-2394

August 21, 1997

Mr. John C. Parker
President
Biotech Research, Inc.
200 Ocean Park Drive
San Diego, CA 17239

Dear Mr. Parker:

I had heard a rumor to the effect that you might be looking for a Director of Research Laboratories at your corporate offices there in San Diego. If this is true, I wanted to let you know of my strong interest in this position.

As Vice President of Technology for BioSci Industries, I direct all research activities of a 110 employee research center engaged in biotechnology research. During my 5 years in this capacity, we have developed and successfully launched over 20 new products accounting for a dramatic increase in annual sales volume ($75 million to $220 million). Additionally, we currently have over 50 key patents pending, which could more than double current sales in less than two years.

Educationally, I hold a Ph.D. in Biochemistry from the University of Southern California and an MBA in Finance & Marketing from Pepperdine University. I have over 20 years experience in biotechnology research, having started as a Research Scientist and advanced through several professional and managerial assignments to my current position.

I am a strong team player, and have developed an excellent reputation for working closely with the marketing and manufacturing functions to rapidly develop and successfully commercialize a number of new products. My interpersonal and communications skills are excellent.

I have long admired the work that BioTech Research has been doing in the field of cancer and virology research, and would welcome the opportunity to join your senior management team as Director of your research effort.

Should you be interested in pursuing my candidacy, I would pleased to meet with you at your convenience. I can be reached at the phone numbers shown on the above letterhead.

Thank you for your consideration.

Sincerely,

William M. Morris

William M. Morris

SAMUEL D. PATTERSON

124 High Street
Fort Wayne, IN 12479

Home: (214) 337-9127
Office: (214) 228-3484

June 23, 1995

Ms. Beverly T. Johnson
Director of Corporate Accounting
Prudential Insurance Company
220 Wacker Drive
Chicago, IL 12485

Dear Ms. Johnson:

If you are looking for a strong General Ledger Accountant for either a corporate or division-level assignment, you may want to consider giving me a call.

I hold a B.S. degree in Accounting from the University of Indiana, and have had four years accounting experience with the Northwestern Insurance Company. Previous experience includes two years as an Auditor with Price Waterhouse, during which time I received my C.P.A.

Currently, I am a Senior Accountant in Northwestern's Corporate Accounting Department. In this capacity I report to the Manager of Corporate Accounting and have functional accountability for reconciliation of general ledger account balances, preparation of monthly profit & loss statements, compliance with external filing requirements and related financial analysis.

I am thoroughly familiar with all aspects of general ledger accounting and associated standard accounting procedures. I am also well-versed in both federal and state filing requirements and work closely with the Corporate Tax Department in preparation of federal, state and local tax returns.

As you may be aware, Northwestern has recently undertaken a massive downsizing effort, reducing the size of its corporate staff by nearly 35%. My position is only one of several hundred positions that the company has elected to eliminate.

If you are looking for someone with my credentials, or if you are aware of any openings outside of Prudential, I would appreciate hearing from you. Thank you for your time and consideration.

Sincerely,

Samuel D. Patterson

SUSAN B. BAILY

180 North Church Road
Boston, MA 16239

Home: (617) 229-3928
Office: (617) 335-9031

September 16, 1997

Mr. Walter R. Lowndry
Chief Financial Officer
Lever Bothers Company
300 Park Avenue
New York, NY 12948

Dear Mr. Lowndry:

I have recently decided to make a career change, and am currently looking for a senior accounting management position at the director or vice presidential level with a major consumer products company. The position I seek could be at either the corporate or division level.

Should you be in the market for a strong accounting executive for a key management position at Lever Brothers, you may want to consider my credentials as follow:

- MBA, Finance, Columbia University
  BS, Accounting, Rutgers University
  CPA, Commonwealth of Pennsylvania

- Key Accounting Management Experience as Follows:

        3 Years = Division Controller, Johnson & Johnson
        2 Years = Director Corp. Accounting, Johnson & Johnson
        3 Years = Manager Corp. Accounting, Johnson & Johnson
        2 Years = Tax Manager, Campbell Soup
        2 Years = Auditing Manager, Campbell Soup
        3 Years = Plant Accountant, Campbell Soup
        2 Years = Sr. Manufacturing Accountant, Campbell Soup
        1 Year = Manufacturing Cost Accountant, Campbell Soup
        2 Years = Auditor, Coopers & Lybrand

My rapid advancement and career progression should provide solid evidence that I have been a strong performer throughout my professional career. Additionally, I have been continuously categorized, by those to whom I have reported, as a charismatic leader with excellent interpersonal and communication skills.

Should this brief summary of my qualifications be of interest to you, I would be very happy to meet with you personally to explore opportunities with your company. I sincerely appreciate your consideration, and look forward to your reply.

Sincerely,

Susan B. Baily

Susan B. Baily

MARY ANNE REED
126 Greentree Lane
Norwalk, CT 23957

April 12, 1996

Mr. Wilbur T. Jackson
Director of Corporate Finance
Bristol Meyers-Squibb Company
100 Lawrenceville Pike
Princeton, NJ 18274

Dear Mr. Jackson:

If you are looking to add a young, experienced Financial Analyst to your staff with strong background in merger and acquisition analysis, you may want to take a close look at my credentials. I have the education and experience that could prove very beneficial to your M&A program:

Please consider the following credentials:

- MBA in Finance, Amos Tuck School, Dartmouth

- BS in Chemical Engineering, Princeton University

- 4 Years experience in merger & acquisitions analysis -
  Standard Brands Company - Corp. Development Department

Key Accomplishments Include:

- Analysis of 16 acquisition candidates

- Development of acquisition analysis computer model
  allowing department to double productivity

- Recommendations resulted in purchase of 4 companies, all
  of which have met or exceeded ROI expectations.

If my qualifications interest you, I would appreciate the opportunity to meet with you to further explore my capabilities and the contributions I could make to Bristol Meyers-Squibb.

I can be reached at my office (Phone: 212-557-0985) during the day or at my home (Phone: 217-558-0978) during evening hours.

Thank you for your consideration.

Sincerely,

Mary Anne Reed

Mary Anne Reed

JUDITH E. PASCHALL
833 Niagara Road
Buffalo, NY 13872

Phone: (315) 779–9048

April 4, 1996

Mr. William Braddock
President
Braddock, Beer & Fletcher, Inc.
105 Executive Row, East
Erie, PA 19238

Dear Mr. Braddock:

Should you be conducting a search for someone with my strong management experience, I would be interested in discussing with you how my abilities may match your clients' needs.

My last position as Vice President of Direct Phone Operations at Vandcourt Investments gave me the opportunity to expand on my many years consulting in the design and implementation of financial and business planning processes. My MBA in Finance from the University of Chicago Business School proved to be a firm foundation upon which to build.

The remainder of my experience has been split between operations and business planning. My undergraduate training in engineering has provided me with the analytical and problem-solving skills to quickly identify critical factors underlying business performance, and design and implement the programs required to improve operations significantly. Over 70% of my experience has involved international operations.

I am seeking a senior finance or business development role with a small to medium-sized company. Target industries include petrochemical, chemical, biotech, high tech, transportation and specialty materials.

My qualifications and experience are strongly multi-functional, giving me the managerial breadth to add considerable value to my employer, especially in dynamic growth or turnaround environments. I would like to talk with you in more detail about the contributions and value I could bring to your clients. I will plan to call you shortly to accomplish this.

Sincerely,

Judith E. Paschall

Judith E. Paschall

PATRICIA A. IPPOLITI

233 Highmeadows Road, Cleveland Heights, OH 14228

May 16, 1996

Mr. James K. Slaughter
Director of Human Resources
Goodyear Company
1200 Avenue of Commerce
Akron, OH 14236

Dear Mr. Slaughter:

I am an experienced employment professional with solid training and experience in recruitment and employment for a Fortune 200 corporation. Please take a brief moment to consider my qualifications as follow:

- MBA, Human Resources Management, Michigan State University.

- BA, Business Administration, University of Wisconsin

- 5 Years Corporate Employment Experience with USX Corp. as follows:

  2 Years = Manager of Technical Employment
  2 Years = Ass't. Manager, Administrative Employment
  1 Year = College Relations Specialist

My employment experience is broad, covering a wide range of business functions including: marketing & sales, manufacturing, engineering, research, accounting & finance, human resources, public affairs, law, management information services, law and logistics. Additionally, I have handled all levels of recruitment from entry level professional through vice president.

I am seeking a senior level management position in employment at the corporate level. Ideally, this would be either Director or Manager of Corporate Employment.

Should you have an appropriate opening on your corporate employment staff, I would appreciate the opportunity to meet with you. My office phone number is (216) 388-9547. Should you wish to reach me in the evening, my home phone is (216) 977-5572.

I look forward to the possibility of talking with you. Thank you for your consideration.

Sincerely,

Patricia A. Ippoliti

Patricia A. Ippoliti

VIRGINIA S. MOORE
155 School House Lane
Wayne, PA 19347

August 15, 1995

Mr. Warren A. Deutsch
President
Deutsch, Shay & Parker Assoc.
1602 Chestnut Street
Philadelphia, PA 19317

Dear Mr. Deutsch:

Some recent changes here at SmithKline Beckman Corporation have prompted my decision to make a confidential career change. I am therefore sending this brief synopsis of my qualifications to your attention in the event one of your clients may be in search of someone with my credentials.

Highlights of my qualifications are as follow:

- Ph.D., Industrial Psychology, Un. of Michigan

- 18 years human resources experience in the consumer products (Colgate Palmolive) and pharmaceutical (SmithKline Beckman) industries

As Director of Human Resources for the Corporate Staff of SmithKline, I currently report to the Senior Vice President of Human Resources and provide a full range of human resource support services to the corporate offices (1,800 employees) of this $7 billion pharmaceutical manufacturer. In this capacity, I direct a staff of 36 employees with functional responsibility for human resources planning, staffing, organization design & development, training, compensation & benefits, and equal opportunity.

I am seeking a senior level human resources management position , preferably at the vice president level, with broad executive leadership responsibility for management of an organization's human resources. Although clearly secondary to job challenge and interest, my compensation requirements (base salary plus bonus) are in the low $100K range.

If this synopsis is of interest, I would be pleased to provide you with a more specific accounting of my qualifications during a face-to-face meeting. Should you wish, I can be reached at my office (Phone: 215-877-2121.)

Thank you.

Sincerely,

Virginia S. Moore
Virginia S. Moore

10 North Canyon Road
Waco, TX 14359

September 22, 1996

Mr. Frank L. Luciano
Director of Corporate Planning
Sun Company
Sun Center
Radnor, PA 19358

Dear Mr. Luciano:

As a corporate planning manager for a major oil and petrochemical company, perhaps you are looking for a talented and accomplished analyst to join your staff. As a Senior Planning Analyst for one of Sun's key competitors, my background could be of particular interest to you.

My overall qualifications include an MBA in Finance from Texas A & M and 4 years experience in the Corporate Planning Department of the EXXON Corporation, where I have worked as both a Planning Analyst and Senior Planning Analyst. Key projects on which I have worked have included:

- Analysis and long range forecast of business growth potential for Lubricants Division

- Study and recommendations concerning feasibility of entering the mass retail market for motor oils

- Economic feasibility study and recommendations on proposed multi-million dollar expansion of the North Fork Refinery

- Numerous "what if" studies to support Executive Committee in preparation of corporate long-range strategic plans

I have consistently achieved high performance evaluations and am recognized as one of the top contributors within the planning department. Additionally, I have frequently been assigned as the lead senior analyst on most of the corporation's key planning projects.

Should you wish to discuss my qualifications further, I can be reached at (214) 665-2149 during the day or (214) 455-2364 during the evening.

I appreciate your consideration, and look forward to the prospect of hearing from you. Thank you.

Sincerely,

James T. Brighton

James T. Brighton

JESUS S. HERNANDEZ

603 Beachaven Road
Ocean Grove, CA 13596

Home: (216) 555-3748
Office:(216) 475-9124

June 27, 1996

Ms. Marjorie B. Walters
Executive Vice President
Stone Container Corporation
600 Tower Hill Drive
San Francisco, CA 13496

Dear Ms. Walters:

I have been watching the rapid growth of Stone Container Corporation over the last 5 years and have been quite impressed with the company's strategic leadership. Your careful positioning in the value-added segment of the market has done much to move you far ahead of competition. Your record has been most impressive!

Two years ago, I left my position as Director of Corporate Planning with Packaging Corporation of America to accept the position of Vice President of Corporate Planning with Transamerica Corporation. Although I have done well in this assignment, I miss the excitement of working for a manufacturing company. Consequently, I have decided to return to the packaging industry and am seeking a senior level position in corporate planning.

My credentials include an MBA in Finance from Stanford University and over 18 years experience in corporate planning and finance. Most of my career has been with PCA, where I advanced rapidly through a series of financial and planning assignments. This included 2 years as Director of Corporate Finance and nearly 4 years as Director of Corporate Planning.

Some of my key accomplishment at PCA have included:

- Successful acquisition of 6 corrugated mills, doubling
  the company's corrugated manufacturing capacity.

- Led company's entry into the laminated bleached board
  market, now the most profitable segment of the business
  (62% of net profits).

- Sale of company's Folding Box Division to Champion
  International Corporation for $960 million (considered a
  major strategic coup).

Perhaps you may be looking for a strong executive to head your planning function. If so, I would welcome the opportunity to meet with you to further explore my qualifications and to discuss the possible contributions I could make to your company.

Thank you for your consideration.

Sincerely,

Jesus S. Hernandez

Jesus S. Hernandez

MICHAEL J. STEVENSON

135 Wellington Avenue
Silver Springs, MD 13958

Home: (216) 377-1284
Office: (216) 374-1938

March 15, 1995

Mr. John B. Farrow
Farrow, Rowe & Harper
205 Wisconsin Avenue
Washington, DC 17385

Dear Mr. Farrow:

As key lobbyists for the tobacco industry, you could well have some interest in my background as a Legislative Affairs Specialist for your firm. Please consider my credentials.

I am a 1991 graduate from the University of Maryland with a Masters degree in Government & Politics. For the past two years, I have been employed as a Legislative Representative for the National Tobacco Manufacturer's Association at the national office here in Washington. In this position I am responsible for representing the interests of the Association with respect to pending legislative matters and working with coalitions of various lobbying interests to influence legislation having impact on the industry.

Some of my key accomplishments have included the following:

- Was the key catalyst in combining the efforts of 12 different associations and lobbying firms to defeat the No Smoking on Public Conveyance Bill.

- Worked with top aids of Senator Harrison's office to re-word the Clean Air Act to minimize its negative effect on the Tobacco Industry.

Prior to this, I worked for two years as a Legislative Assistant to Senator John Thornton. In this capacity, I was heavily involved in researching and drafting key legislation which the Senator wished to support. In addition, I worked behind the scenes to solicit senatorial support and align a variety of political forces in support of sponsored legislation.

I feel my political connections, coupled with my knowledge of the inner workings of the political system, could prove quite valuable to a lobbying consulting firm such as yours.

Should you agree, I would welcome the opportunity to meet with you to explore how I might fit into your organization. Thank you for your consideration, and I look forward to hearing from you.

Sincerely,

Michael J. Stevenson

Michael J. Stevenson

DAVID C. McCARTHY

305 Old Saddle Road   Home: (215) 874-1837
Malvern, PA 12837   Office:(215) 874-2198

October 28, 1997

Mr. Gordon B. Silcox
Silcox, Waters & Smart, Inc.
Executive Search Consultants
826 Park Avenue
New York, NY 18348

Dear Mr. Silcox:

I did not wish to bore you by sending yet another unsolicited resume to your attention. Instead, this letter will serve to briefly highlight my credentials so that you can ascertain the appropriateness of my qualifications for current search assignments on which you may now be working.

I hold an M.A. in English (communications emphasis) from Northwestern University and have over 20 years experience in the field of Public Affairs. A brief summary of recent experience follows:

    5 Years - Vice President Public Affairs, Commodore Computers
    3 Years - Director of Communications, Franklin Mint
    4 Years - Manager Employee Communications, DuPont Company

The current economic turmoil at Commodore, coupled with the frequent changes of company president, have prompted my decision to seek employment in a more stable environment.

I am seeking a senior executive level position in Public Affairs in a medium-sized or major corporation, which has demonstrated a solid record of growth and financial performance. My compensation requirements are in the $125,000 to $135,000 range, and I am open to geographical relocation.

Should you have a client who has a need for a seasoned Public Affairs executive, I would welcome your call. Should our conversation lead to continued interest, I would be pleased to furnish you with a complete copy of my resume at that time.

Thank you for considering my qualifications, and I look forward to hearing from you should you have an appropriate assignment that fits my background and interests.

Sincerely,

David C. McCarthy

David C. McCarthy

LINDA B. JENKINS
20 Lingren Circle
Stevens Point, WI 17354

September 21, 1994

Mr. James D. Farrington, Esq.
Farrington & Associates
Attorneys at Law
306 Riverview Road
Green Bay, WI 13957

Dear Mr. Farrington:

A recent graduate of the University of Wisconsin School of Law with over 4 years previous experience as a Law Clerk for the corporate legal department of Kimberly-Clark Corporation, I am ready for my first assignment as a practicing attorney. Please consider my credentials as follow:

- J.D., University of Wisconsin School of Law, (With Honors)

- B.S., Political Science, University of Wisconsin, (Cum Laude)

- 4 Years, Law Clerk, Kimberly-Clark Corporation

During my employment with Kimberly-Clark, I worked in two areas of law. Three of these years were spent doing patent research and handling a portion of the patent filing process under the direction of Martin H. Sweeney, Corporate Patent Attorney. The remaining year was spent doing providing research and support to William Kursner in the area of consumer litigation.

My educational background and work experience with Kimberly-Clark have provided me with a solid foundation upon which to build a successful career in the practice of law. I would like to begin my career with a private law practice such as yours where, through hard work and contribution to the firm, I might eventually have the opportunity to advance to the position of Partner.

Should you be looking for a well-educated and ambitious young attorney to join your firm, I would welcome the opportunity to meet with you to explore this possibility. With my drive and motivation to succeed, I know that I can make a substantive contribution to the firm.

My home telephone number is (214) 779-2641. Thank you for your consideration, and I look forward to hearing from you.

Sincerely,

Linda B. Jenkins

Linda B. Jenkins

THOMAS J. FOSTER
201 Mountain View Road
Raleigh, NC 18476

March 26, 1997

Ms. Barbara R. Thompson
President
Thompson, King & Lamar
Suite 330 Executive Towers
211 Newmarket Parkway
Marietta, GA 30067

Dear Ms. Thompson:

Should one of your client corporations be searching for a Vice President and General Counsel, you may want to consider my credentials. Some highlights of my qualifications are:

- LL.B., University of Virginia School of Law

- Direct 25 person corporate law department for $1.5 billion electronic components manufacturer

- Over 20 years corporate law experience with major corporations

In my current position as General Counsel for Franklin Electronics, I report to the President and am responsible for all legal matters pertaining to the operation of this $1.5 billion corporation.

Some of my major achievements include:

- Settlement of a $120 million government contract law suit for $18 million on an out-of-court basis.

- Won major antitrust case which would have required divestiture of most profitable division.

- Defeated major class action suit that would have cost government contracts valued at $85 million.

My current annual compensation is $145,000 ($120,000 base salary plus $25,000 executive bonus). In addition, I qualify for stock options and am provided with a company car.

Should you feel one of your clients may have an interest in my background, I would welcome the opportunity to talk with you. I can be reached at my office -- phone (236) 991-0785.

Thank you.

Sincerely,

Thomas J. Foster

Thomas J. Foster

MARSUE S. CASTELLENTE

20 Cider Mill Road, Portland, OR 84720

June 22, 1997

Mr. David C. Jansen
MIS Manager
Rawlings Corporation
235 Oxford Road
Tacoma, WA 43958

Dear Mr. Jansen:

I recently learned that you are installing Novello System 200 at your corporate offices in Tacoma. I have been Project Manager for the successful installation and start-up of this same system at Warrington Mills here in Portland, and could be a valuable asset to your project.

Some highlights of my career include:

- B.S., Computer Science, University of Washington

- 5 Years MIS experience with Warrington Mills as follows:

      1 Year = Project Manager, Novello System 200
      2 Years = Senior Analyst, Human Resource Systems
      1 Year = Analyst, Accounting Systems
      1 Year = Programmer/Analyst, General Support

For your general information, Novello System 200 poses a particular challenge since certain key documentation is missing. Additionally, some of the functionality which Novello lists in its product specification is simply nonfunctional and needs debugging.

If you are interested in hiring an experienced Novello System 200 Project Leader who has been on the "bleeding edge of technology", you may want to give me a call. I can probably save you many weeks of installation time and a lot of stress and frustration.

Should you wish to contact me, I can be reached at (216) 877-9572. Thank you for your consideration.

Sincerely,

Marsue S. Castellente

Marsue S. Castellente

WARREN H. JAMES
824 Kingman Lane
Forest Hills, NY 18347

June 16, 1996

Mr. William B. Carter
Senior Vice President
Corporate Administration
General Instrument Corporation
810 East 42nd Street
New York, NY 18476

Dear Mr. Carter:

Some recent management changes at Rockwell International have prompted my decision to seek a career change. This decision is highly confidential, and senior management is unaware of my intention. I am seeking a senior executive level position in MIS management with a major high-technology manufacturer.

Highlights of my qualifications are as follow:

- MBA, University of Connecticut

- B.S., Computer Science, Georgia Tech

- 26 Years MIS experience, with most recent career
  assignments as follow:

        5 Years = Vice President MIS, Rockwell International
        2 Years = Director of MIS, Rockwell International
        2 Years = Manager MIS Operation, IBM Corporation
        1 Year = Manger Client Services, IBM Corporation

In my current position as Vice President MIS at Rockwell, I report to the Executive Vice President - Administration, and have responsibility for directing a 240 person MIS function with operating and administrative budget of $43 million. Some key accomplishments include:

- Successful installation and start-up of $20 million, corporate-wide general
  ledger system

- Successful installation and start-up of $18 million, corporate-wide, totally
  integrated order entry & tracking/production & inventory scheduling/
  purchasing system

I have enjoyed an excellent reputation for timely delivery of state-of-the-art MIS systems that have greatly improved management decision-making efficiency and company productivity, at highly competitive costs. Excellent references are readily available.

Should you have an interest in my qualifications, I can be reached at (212) 879-5127. Thank you for your consideration.

Sincerely,

Warren H. James

Warren H. James

ERNEST M. WILLIAMS
125 Elm Avenue
Cherry Hill, NJ 18375

September 14, 1996

Mr. Calvin C. Jones
Manager of Distribution
Sterling Drug Company
20 Great Valley Parkway
Malvern, PA 19356

Dear Mr. Jones:

I recently read about Sterling's plan to construct a 900,000 square foot manufacturing and distribution facility in Montgomery County. This suggests that you may shortly be in need of experienced distribution professionals. If so, please consider my qualifications as follow:

- B.A., Business Administration, Temple University

- 4 Years Distribution Center Management Experience as as Follows:

      1 Year = Distribution Center Manager
             Campbell Soup Company, Camden, NJ

      2 Years = Warehouse Supervisor
             Campbell Soup Company, Camden, NJ

      1 Year = Shipping Expeditor
             Campbell Soup Company, Camden, NJ

Some key contributions have included:

- 1 year carrier study, resulting in major shift from truck to rail shipments (18% annual cost savings)

- Improved production efficiency by 12% and decreased product damage by 65% through reconfiguration of high volume product storage pattern to reduce product handling

I have been watching Sterling's impressive growth, and would very much like to have the chance to explore employment opportunities with your firm. I am hopeful, therefore, that I will be hearing from you.

I can be reached at (609) 665-9070. Thank you for your consideration.

Sincerely

Ernest M. Williams

Ernest M. Williams

316 Round Tree Road
Stanford, CT 16385

August 21, 1995

Mr. John K. Keery
Executive Vice President
Distribution & Logistics
General Foods Corporation
General Foods Towers
White Plains, NY 37286

Dear Mr. Keery:

If you are in search of a strong candidate for a senior level Logistics management position with your corporate staff or one of your larger divisions, you may want to take a moment to consider my credentials. My background in the consumer goods industry, coupled with significant contributions in the Logistics area, may well be of interest to you.

Currently corporate Director of Logistics for the Colgate Palmolive Company, I direct a staff of 65 employees responsible for management of all Logistics activities for this $2.8 billion dollar consumer goods manufacturer on a world-wide basis. Functional responsibility includes: production planning and scheduling, purchasing, scheduling and management of raw materials inventories, and warehousing & distribution management.

My credentials include a Masters degree in Distribution Management from University of Tennessee and a B.S. degree in Industrial Engineering from Purdue University. I have 22 years experience in Logistics and Logistics management at two major companies (Colgate Palmolive and Procter & Gamble), and have held a series of progressively responsible management positions in most functional areas which comprise the Logistics area.

I have had a strong history of being a key contributor to overall business strategy, and have implemented numerous programs resulting in millions of dollars of savings to my employers. I also enjoy an excellent reputation as a manager and leader of people. Interpersonal and communication skills are also strong points.

I would appreciate the opportunity to meet with you and other appropriate members of your senior management team to explore how I might fit into your organization, and to discuss the potential contributions I could make to your company. Should you wish to explore this matter, I can be reached at (212) 427-5125.

Thank you for your consideration.

Sincerely,

Lou Ann Atkinson

Lou Ann Atkinson

PHYLLIS J. CHEYNEY

201 Stoney Brook Road   Home: (603) 997-0138
Wilbraham, MA 39572   Office:(603) 775-3264

November 22, 1996

Mr. Fulton T. Barry
Director of Quality
Monsanto Chemical Company
125 Chemical Road
Springfield, MA 39547

Dear Mr. Barry:

If you are currently in the market for an outstanding candidate for a
Quality management position at Monsanto, you will likely have an interest
in my qualifications. Please consider the following credentials:

- B.S. Degree, Industrial Engineering, Un. of Massachusetts

- Certified Quality Engineer, A.S.Q.C., 1994

- Regional Chairperson, A.S.Q.C., Northeast Region (2 Years)

- Total Quality Education:

        Dr. G. Edwards Deming Seminar, 1993
        Crosby Quality College Graduate, 1992
        Statistical Process Control, Un. of Tennessee, 1991
        Introduction to Quality Statistics, 1991

- 6 Years Quality Management Experience with Polaroid
  Corporation as Follows:

        2 Years = Quality Manager, Framingham Plant
        2 Years = Ass't. Quality Manager, Corporate Offices
        2 Years = Quality Associate, Corporate Offices

I have strong background in the design and implementation of SPC-based
total quality initiatives in chemical process manufacturing facilities, and
am up-to-date with most leading-edge quality concepts and approaches. My
knowledge and leadership have earned me solid recognition at Polaroid as
well as external recognition by A.S.Q.C., where I now serve as Chairperson
for the Northeast Region.

Should you have an interest in my background and wish to further explore my
possible candidacy, I can be reached at the phone numbers shown in the
above letterhead.

Thank you for your consideration.

                                    Sincerely,

                                    Phyllis J. Cheyney

                                    Phyllis J. Cheyney

MARTHA B. HILLER

625 Walnut Lane, Wyomissing, PA 13496

October 4, 1994

Mr. William H. Harbster
Vice President of Operations
Carpenter Technology, Inc.
300 River Road
Reading, PA 19347

Dear Mr. Harbster:

I am a well-seasoned, knowledgeable quality executive with a strong background in the metals industry. I am seeking a position at the Director or Vice President level with a progressive metals industry manufacturer that is looking for strong leadership in the corporate-wide implementation of a total quality initiative.

Please consider my credentials:

- B.S. Degree, Mechanical Engineering, Penn State University

- Certified Quality Engineer, American Society of Quality Control

- 15 Years Experience in the Quality Field Which Includes:

> 4 Years = Director of Quality, Reading Tube Corp.
> 5 Years = Manager of Quality, Reading Tube Corp.
> 2 Years = Quality Supervisor, Specialty Metals, Inc.
> 1 Year = Sr. Quality Engineer, Specialty Metals, Inc.
> 3 Years = Quality Engineer, Specialty Metals, Inc.

In my current position as Director of Quality at Reading Tube Corporation, I have led the design and implementation of a highly successful SPC-based total quality program on a corporate-wide basis. This included the corporate staff and the company's 3 manufacturing sites (1 refinery and 2 tube manufacturing plants). This program has cut customer complaints by 92% and reduced scrap by more than 80%. Estimated annual savings of this major initiative is in the $15 to $20 million range.

Should you have an interest in my qualifications, please feel free to contact me at my office --- (215) 775-2948.

Thank you for your consideration, and I look forward to hearing from you.

Sincerely,

Martha B. Hiller

Martha B. Hiller

KEVIN B. HARBSTER
120 Eagle Woods Road
Wilmington, DL 17239

October 22, 1997

Mr. Craig H. Johnston
Director of Procurement
Scott Paper Company
Scott Plaza
Philadelphia, PA 19113

Dear Mr. Johnston:

As you are probably aware, the DuPont Company has recently announced a cutback in the size of its Wilmington-based workforce by some 4,000 employees. My position, unfortunately, was one of many that have been eliminated by the company.

Should you be on the market for talented, young Procurement Manager for either a corporate or division-level assignment, I would welcome the opportunity to speak with you.

A brief summary of my qualifications follows:

- B.S., Chemical Engineering, University of Delaware

- 4 Years Corporate Procurement Experience as Follows:

    1 Year = Manager Engineering Procurement
    1 Year = Senior Buyer - Engineering
    1 Year = Buyer - Specialty Chemicals
    1 Year = Assoc. Buyer - Packaging Supplies

As you can see, I have had a broad smattering of purchasing experience across a wide range of products (most of a fairly technical nature). My experience includes the responsibility for the negotiation and management of multi-million dollar national contracts supplying some 50 DuPont manufacturing sites. Major contracts that I have handled include those at the $100+ million level.

During my 4 years with DuPont, I have been credited with savings in the $10 to $15 million range. These have come about principally as the result of a combination of skillful negotiations and exhaustive research to identify new, more competitive supply sources. Perhaps I could bring similar results to your company.

Should you wish to further explore my background and credentials, please call me at (302) 775-9075. I can be reached between the hours of 8:00 AM and 5:30 PM.

Thank you for your consideration.

Sincerely,

Kevin B. Harbster

Kevin B. Harbster

AGNES B. OWENS

233 Sharon Lane, Rockford, IL 14567

May 2, 1996

Mr. Samuel P. Richter
President
Richter Chemical Company
155 West Carlton Street
Chicago, IL 32497

Dear Mr. Richter:

I recently read an article in the *Chicago Tribune* about the enormous success of Richter Chemical Company in the field of specialty chemicals and the major expansion you are planning. I would very much like to be a part of your future plans, and feel I have much to offer a company such as yours as a senior procurement officer.

My qualifications include:

- B.S., Chemistry, Ohio State University

- MBA, Finance, Northwestern University

- 20 Years Procurement Experience in the Chemical Industry

  3 Years = Vice President Procurement, Barlow Chemical
  2 Years = Director of Procurement, Barlow Chemical
  3 Years = Manager Raw Materials Purchasing, Dow Chemical
  2 Years = Manager Chemicals Purchasing, Dow Chemical
10 Years = Various Purchasing Assignments, Dow Chemical

My twenty years of professional and managerial experience as a procurement professional in the chemical industry has prepared me well for a high growth company such as yours. I am up-to-date on the latest procurement systems and processes and could provide excellent strategic leadership to your procurement function. I have always enjoyed a strong reputation as an innovator who knows how to create and manage a procurement function that returns significant savings to the business.

Perhaps it may be worth your while to meet with me and explore the many ways in which I could save your company time and money. If you agree, I can be reached at (235) 726-9083.

Thank you for your consideration, and I look forward to hearing from you.

Sincerely,

Agnes B. Owens

Agnes B. Owens

RONALD K. SCHULTZ
135 Kelly Drive
West Reading, PA 19457
(215) 774-9125

February 22, 1994

Dr. Walter S. Klein
Director of Technology
KDF Micrographics, Inc.
200 River Road
Reading, PA 19459

Dear Dr. Klein:

I am a Research Engineer with 6 years experience in the development of photoimaging products used in the microprocessing field. Currently a key contributor to James River Graphics' research effort in the micrographics field, my key achievements include:

- Lead researcher in the development of JRG's
  revolutionary new TEP microfilm technology

- Development of new non-silver halide film
  technology for use in consumer photographic
  market

- Development of novel, new updatable microfiche
  for use in microfilm files

My technical qualifications include:

- Ph.D., Polymer Science, M.I.T., 1988
  M.S., Chemical Engineering, R.P.I., 1986
  B.S., Chemical Engineering, Un. of Mass., 1984

- 6 years R & D product and process development in
  photoimaging technology

- Awarded 18 U.S. patents on new photoimaging products
  and technology, with an additional 15 patent disclosures

I am seeking a position as a Group Leader or Research Manager with responsibility for direction of a product development team in the field of photoimaging-related research. Compensation requirements are in the $75,000 to $80,000 range, and I am open to relocation to most areas of the country.

Should my credentials be of interest to KDF Micrographics, I would appreciate hearing from you. I can be reached at my home number most week nights after 7:00 PM.

Thank you for your consideration, and I look forward to hearing from you.

Sincerely,

Ronald K. Schultz

Ronald K. Schultz

MARY ANNE WADSWORTH

324 Silver Lake Road
Racine, WI 13243

Home: (313) 674-1736
Office: (313) 678-3425

July 23, 1997

Mr. Scott T. Michaelson
Michaelson & Jansen, Inc.
205 Fox River Blvd.
Green Bay, WI 13458

Dear Mr. Michaelson:

Perhaps one of your current clients is in need of a senior accounting manager for their corporate accounting operations. If so, they may well have an interest in my qualifications as follow:

Educational Qualifications:

- B.A., Accounting, University of Wisconsin, 1990
  M.B.A., Finance, Michigan State University, 1992
  C.P.A., State of Wisconsin, June 1991

Professional Experience:

- 2 years Public Accounting experience - Price Waterhouse
- 5 years experience - Kimberly-Clark Corp. as follows:

  1 Year = Assistant Manager - Corporate Accounting
  2 Years = Manager - General Ledger Accounting
  1 Year = Accounting Supervisor
  1 Year = Senior Accountant

I am seeking a position as Manager or Director of Corporate Accounting for a major manufacturing company with direct reporting relationship to the Chief Financial Officer. My compensation requirements are in the $80,000 to $90,000 range, and I am willing to relocate for the right opportunity.

I have an excellent performance record, and am considered to be a "high potential" employee by my current employer. Unfortunately, I do not see the opportunity for advancement in the foreseeable future. Outstanding references are readily available upon request.

If I appear to be a match for any of your current search assignments, I would welcome the opportunity to meet with you and will provide you with a complete summary of my qualifications at that time.

Thank you for your consideration.

Sincerely,

Mary Anne Wadsworth

Mary Anne Wadsworth

DAVID T. BARNES
85 Coventree Lane
Oklahoma City, OK 43547
(317) 552-1323

March 12, 1995

Mr. Sidney F. Winehouse
National Sales Manager
U.S. Hardware Supply, Inc.
400 Canyon Highway, SE
Tulsa, OK 43857

Dear Mr. Winehouse:

What would you give to be able to hire one of the top sales representatives of your largest competitor? This is your chance!

I am currently the leading Senior Accounts Representative for the Southwest Region of Lone Star Hardware Supply. Major accomplishments include:

- National Sales Award - 1995, 94, 93, 92 & 91
  (top 10% of sales representatives nationally)

- Sales Rep of the Year Award - Southwest Region -
  1994, Runner Up - 1993

- Increased territory sales volume by 600% in
  5 years

I have been very impressed with your new Krafts Handtool line as well as other new hardware lines you have introduced during the last two years. I feel that I could have major impact on your sales volume if given the opportunity to manage your Western Region. With my proven sales ability and your quality products and competitive pricing, I feel certain that I could lead U.S. Hardware Supply to the number one competitor in the West in less then two (2) years time!

Hopefully you can see the potential for an excellent marriage here, and will give me a call. I would welcome the opportunity to meet with you to discuss the potential for making a significant contribution to your business. Of course, this inquiry is made in strictest confidence.

Thank you for your consideration, and I look forward to the possibility of meeting with you personally.

Sincerely,

David T. Barnes

David T. Barnes

CAROLYN A. CRISWELL

203 Green Willow Road, West Chester, Pa 19382

May 2, 1995

Mr. James D. Young
Director of Marketing
Finley Tea Company
605 Delaware Avenue
Philadelphia, PA 19117

Dear Mr. Young:

Could your company use a talented, young Brand Manager who has an excellent record of achieving major increases in sales volume through creative marketing approaches in the consumer products industry? If so, you may want to consider bringing me in for an exploratory interview.

Please consider the following credentials:

. M.B.A., Marketing, Wharton School, 1990

. B.A., Business Administration, Penn State, 1987

. 5 Years Marketing Experience - Kraft Foods, Inc.

       2 Years = Senior Brand Manager
       2 Years = Brand Manager
       1 Year = Associate Brand Manager

Key accomplishments include:

. Led national marketing roll-out of new Krispy Bacon Bits line, achieving 60% of market share in less than 2 years.

. Revitalized sagging Swiss cheese line with change in name and packaging coupled with creative advertising theme (55% increase in sales volume in less than 6 months).

. Increased market share of cocktail cracker product line by 33 points to become brand market leader in one year.

I am confident that I can make similar contributions to Finley Tea Company, and would welcome the opportunity to meet with you to explore the potential for a profitable career relationship.

Should you have an interest in my credentials, I can be reached at (215) 431-1436 during week nights.

Thank you for your consideration, and I look forward to hearing from you.

Sincerely,

Carolyn A. Criswell

Carolyn A. Criswell

ROBERT H. HARLOWE
433 Old Oak Road
Augusta, ME 42345
(513) 774-9857

April 23, 1996

Ms. Wilma R. Stevens
The Stevens Group
208 East Wilbraham Road
Springfield, MA 17593

Dear Ms. Stevens:

As an employment agency specializing in the field of Public Affairs, you may wish to be aware of my candidacy. Perhaps one of your client companies is looking for a talented professional with expertise in governmental and legislative affairs.

I hold a B.S. degree in Political Science from American University and have over 5 years experience in the field of governmental and legislative affairs with New England Telephone Company.

In my current position as Manager of Legislative Affairs for the states of Maine, New Hampshire and Massachusetts, I am responsible for the management of a staff of three professionals and am accountable for all state legislative matters affecting the business of New England Telephone Company.

Some key accomplishments include:

- Led lobby effort that defeated Bill 334226 requiring
  a 3% Massachusetts state sales tax surcharge on all
  local toll phone calls (annual savings $26 million).

- Initiated sponsorship and led successful lobby effort
  to pass Bill 44.5578 A (State of Maine), allowing
  New England Telephone to provide long distance services
  within the state (annual sales revenue potential of
  $18 to $20 million in next 5 years).

- Defeated New Hampshire House Bill 1996-344A, requiring
  the replacement of telephone and utility poles every 15
  years (annual savings = $9 million).

Should you feel that one of your current search assignments is a suitable match for my qualifications, I would appreciate hearing from you. I can be reached most evenings at my home between the hours of 7:30 and 9:30 PM.

Thank you for your consideration.

Sincerely,

Robert H. Harlowe

Robert H. Harlowe

CORTLAND T. HARRIS

225 Welcome Drive
Bristol, CT 14567

Home: (213) 877-2234
Office: (213) 775-0956

May 20, 1996

Mr. Douglas M. Deerfield
Vice President Manufacturing
Milton Bradley Company
Route 53
Wilton, CT 18374

Dear Mr. Deerfield:

The Milton Bradley Company has always enjoyed an excellent reputation as one of the area's outstanding employers, and I have long had an interest in working for your company. Perhaps my dream has the potential to become reality!

I understand that Tom Hardy, Operations Manager at your Wilton Plant, has just announced his retirement and that you are about to begin a search for his replacement. Perhaps I could save you the time! Please consider my qualifications for this position:

- MBA, Finance, University of Connecticut, 1986
  B.S., Mechanical Engineering, R.P.I., 1984

- Currently Plant Manager for Karlton's Bristol Plant -
  a 350 employee toy manufacturing facility

- Previously spent 4 years as Operations Manager for
  same facility

- Fully versed in modern manufacturing concepts and
  approaches including JIT, MRP, high performance work
  systems, total quality, etc.

Since assuming the position of Plant Manager at Karlton a year ago, I have brought significant improvements as follow:

- Reduced operating costs by 23% ($4 million annual
  savings)

- Successfully thwarted major union organizing attempt

- Led quality initiative with resultant 68% reduction in
  consumer complaints

I am confident I could make similar contributions to Milton Bradley, and would welcome the opportunity to meet with you personally to explore this possibility.

Thank you, and I look forward to hearing from you shortly.

Sincerely,

Cortland T. Harris

Cortland T. Harris

Index